Th

MW01616776

to

_____

ISBN: 0-9793892-5-9

CREDITS:
Cover Photographs:
Matthew Bosje, Greg Rood, Jane Grafton
Cover Design and Page Layout:
Linda Stubblefield
Proofreaders:
Rena Fish, Jane Grafton, Diane Rykhus, Cindy Schaap

All Scripture references used in this book
are from the King James Bible.

Printed and Bound in the United States

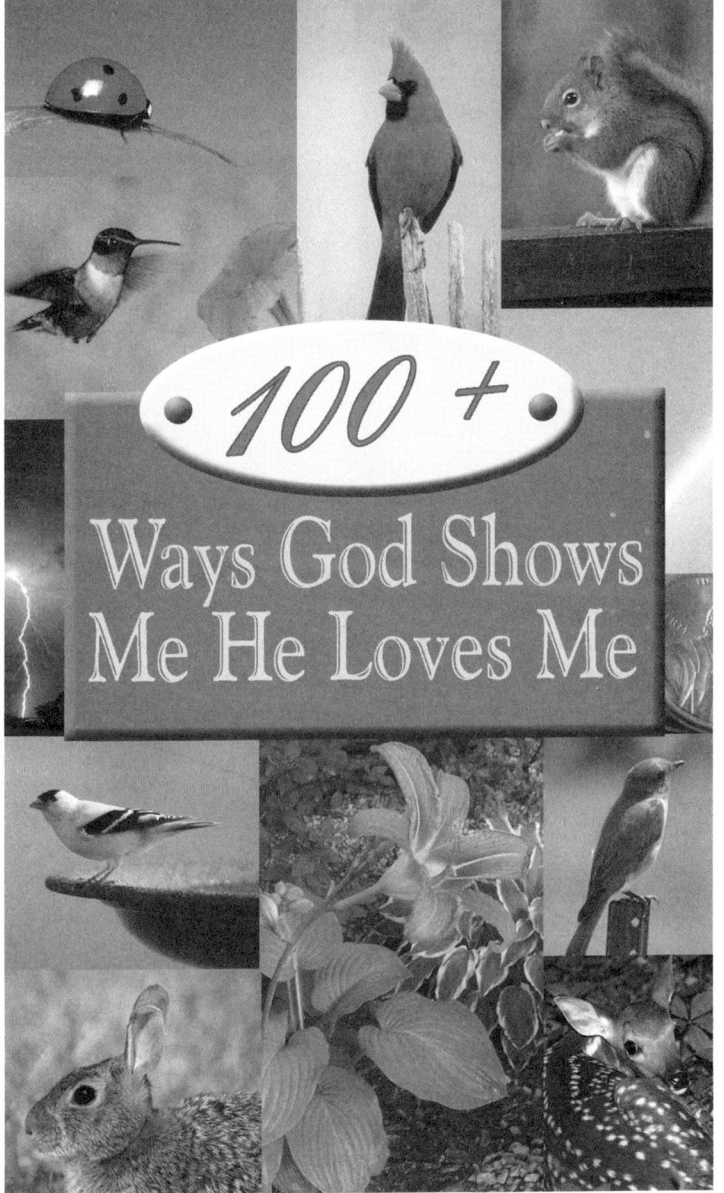

100 +
Ways God Shows
Me He Loves Me

"For the Father
himself loveth you...."

— John 16:27

Acknowledgments

This book would not be possible without the combined efforts of several people who spent time seeking some wonderful stories of God's love for this book. A special thank you to Renee Cox, Marcia Schearer, Linda Vaprezsan, and Amy Vassak. These ladies went above and beyond the call of duty in helping us with this project.

I would also like to thank each dear lady who took the time to write her story and submit it for this book. We are also grateful to those who submitted photographs for us to use on the cover.

*"The whole secret
to the Christian life
is hinged on how much
you believe
God loves you."*

— Dr. Jack Schaap

Introduction

I challenge you to make it a lifelong adventure to learn how much God loves you. My husband teaches that there are several "satellites" that God uses to testify of His reality and of His love for us.

1. **Enjoy nature and God's creation.** When you see something you enjoy in nature, recognize it as a sign of God's love for you. Tell God you love Him and that you know He loves you. God uses all of nature to draw His people to Him. God says that His people are "His portion" ["All He really wants"]. Everything else that belongs to God is used to draw us to Him because God really loves us. Deuteronomy 32:9, *"For the Lord's portion is his people.…"*

2. **Read the Bible daily.** Memorize verses that tell how much God loves you. Do a Bible study on the love of God. There is no need to feel rejected. You are deeply loved by the best that there is!

3. **Be faithful to your local church.** Listen to your pastor as he preaches to you about the One Who will never reject you.

4. **Watch other Christians who know how to express love.** Study their lives and their marriages. Read their books. Learn how to express love from them.

Though I have been dearly loved all of my life, I plan to study the love of God for the rest of my life. I know God is the only loved One Who is 100 percent faithful and that His love is fully satisfying.

The following pages include over 100 stories of the many different ways God showed His love to ladies around the world from all different walks of life. May these many ideas provoke you to look more diligently to find the ways God demonstrates His love for you!

– Cindy Schaap

Preface

$\mathcal{A}$s you read *100+ Ways God Shows Me He Loves Me*, you will find that some stories are more usual, everyday happenings. We wanted to share these stories with you because we want to help you be aware of God and His constant reminders of His love to us in the day-to-day routines of life. While some of the stories are as simple as finding a penny, you will also find that some of the stories are more spectacular; some, such as Marie Bennett's story (# 41) are truly heart-wrenching. I trust you will take the time to read both the simple and the spectacular stories.

I hope that through this book you can find the simple demonstrations of God's love to you and that you can also learn from examples such as Marie Bennett that God loves you even with something happens that is as devastating as both of your children being taken to Heaven in a fatal car crash. If Marie Bennett can praise God, so can you and I.

It is our prayer that this book motivates all of us to praise God and be aware of His many reminders of His love on a daily basis!

– Cindy Schaap

1

*F*or several months, I had the idea of visiting John (my dad's favorite nurse) in his home. John is the man who walked my dad to surgery. He was the last person my dad recognized on this earth. John was the last person to whom my dad spoke; Dad said, "I love you, John," as he was wheeled into the operating room.

My husband thought he knew where John lived, but I had never taken the time to go by and check. On Tuesday, November 26, four days before my birthday, I saw John at my grocery store. I yelled his name, but he left without ever hearing me. A grocery bagger stopped me. This boy seemed to be mentally handicapped, and though I had seen him several times before, I had never spoken to him.

The grocery bagger asked, "Do you know that man?"

"Yes," I answered, "He was my dad's nurse when he was in the hospital."

"Do you know what I think you should do?" he replied, "I think you should find out where he lives and go by and see him."

My husband has said that if Jesus were to come to visit our church, he felt Christ might come in the body of an educable slow person or in the body of a particularly irritating person. I have kept his statement in mind, and I have always tried to be nice to everyone.

I felt my husband was proven right. I knew that God had sent me a message by the tongue of the mentally handicapped grocery bagger. Though I am generally not a spooky person, I walked away from that boy and immediately prayed, "Okay, Lord, I'll go by and witness to John." I asked myself when my next scheduled visitation day was. It was the following Saturday, which was also my birthday. "The Lord wants me to win John to the Lord on my birthday," I thought.

On the Saturday morning of my birthday, I got up, got dressed, and straightened the house. I canceled with my regular soul-winning partners, and around noon, I drove to the house I thought was John's. A woman answered the door.

"I am looking for a man named John who was my dad's nurse at the University of Chicago Hospitals."

"That's my husband," the lady replied, "He just left for the post office, but he'll be back soon if you would like to wait."

I waited in the kitchen and had coffee with John's wife. Eventually, I asked her what she was trusting to get her to Heaven. She said she was trusting her faith in Jesus Christ. She told me she is Methodist, but John is Catholic. I waited 15 minutes, and afraid I was going to wear out my welcome, I started to leave. As soon as I headed for the door, John got home.

I sat at the kitchen table and talked about my dad for several minutes. Then I asked John if I could share my dad's faith with him. People were coming and going in the kitchen, so I did not try to pray with John. I just shook his hand and asked him to promise me that he would pray and accept Christ before he went to bed that night.

I had a box of chocolates for John and his family, so I told John I would go to the car and get them for him before I left. John offered to walk me to my car. I prayed with John in his driveway, and he accepted Christ as his Saviour. What did I learn from this incident?

- Jesus reveals Himself to us through all types of people, so we should be nice to everyone. I was again reminded of one of the most important lessons my dad taught me, "God is no respecter of persons."
- Jesus reveals Himself to those who are grieving. God has been so real in my life; I feel like I can almost reach out and touch Him.
- Jesus reveals Himself to those who walk with Him through Bible reading and prayer.
- Jesus reveals Himself through soul winning. God has shown Himself to me through several avenues. However, many of my most exciting blessings revolve around soul-winning experiences I have had since my dad died.
- The more we follow God's leading, the more we will see His working.

To be honest with you, I was afraid to go to visit John that day. I was afraid to take anyone with me, and I was afraid to go alone. I told my friend on the phone that day that, though I was scared, I knew the worst feeling would be not to act upon what I thought God was asking me to do. I knew God wanted me to witness to John on my birthday. I felt that being rejected would be much better than wondering what might have happened if I had not followed God.

On my last birthday with my dad, he gave me several cards. In 2001 I celebrated my first birthday without my father. I had kept the cards he gave me on my last birthday. I took those cards out and read them and thought to myself, "I won't be getting any more birthday presents from my dad." But I was wrong...

Though I give God all the glory for John's salvation, I felt that John's salvation was my birthday present from my dad. When I spoke with my grocery bagger messenger, I felt that my dad could not be far away.

I returned home to meet my husband and son for a birthday celebration at a restaurant called Meyer's Castle. I opened gifts from those I love until I felt spoiled rotten. But my favorite birthday gift that year arrived around noon. Its arrival was predicted four days before.

Was I rejoicing on my forty-third birthday? You bet I was! Did I miss my dad on my second birthday without him? Somehow it seemed that he was not that far away...and the presence of God seemed closer than ever before.

– Cindy Schaap

When everyone seemed to be picking an item or circumstance that reminds them of God's love, I also wanted to choose one. I had a very difficult time deciding because so very many things remind me of God's love. There are two things that specifically remind me of God's love: (1) Sparrows. I am the mother of a very busy two year old. So many times the kitchen sink is where I do a lot of meditating and praying and thinking. I have a window there with several bird feeders. When I see a sparrow, I am reminded of how God said that a sparrow does not fall without His knowing and that I am of more value than many sparrows. I feel very special and loved by God when I see one.

(2) Squirrels. I know they are considered rodents, but I wanted to choose something that I see very frequently because I feel that I need to be reminded of God's love very often! They are so fun to watch—busy with work and play. They remind me of God's love.

All of nature is God's saying, "I love you, Maria." I am having so much fun showing my son John what God has made. When asked "Who made you?" he now says, "Dee-dus" (meaning "Jesus"). Then we say, "Who loves you?" and he says, "Dee-dus." What a simple thing, but I hope he never forgets!

– Maria Sarver

Mrs. Cindy Schaap was invited to speak at our ladies' retreat. She began to tell how that every time she sees a hummingbird she is reminded of God's love. She happens to **love** hummingbirds. As she was explaining this, one of our ladies, whose name is Stacy, thought to herself, "I hate hummingbirds. In fact, I'm scared of hummingbirds. That certainly would not be a way that I could know God loves me." As Mrs. Schaap was teaching, Stacy began to think of what she liked so that she could be reminded that God loves her. "I love hearts," Stacy said to herself. "I'm going to ask God to give me some heart clouds."

After the retreat, she began to watch the sky whenever she was outside. She just knew God was going to give her some heart clouds. As she was mowing her grass and talking to God one day, she looked up and sure enough, God had placed some cute, heart-shaped clouds in the sky for her! "God," Stacy said, "I know You love me!"

When God gave her more heart-shaped clouds another day, she was so ecstatic that she ran in the house, got her camera, and took pictures of them. She went to Wal-Mart and made copies for all of the church ladies to see. I put my copy in a frame, and I think of Stacy every time I look at it.

Then I began to think, "If God can give Cindy Schaap hummingbirds and Stacy heart-shaped clouds, then I will ask God for something specific too." I decided to ask God for cross clouds. Why I asked for that, I will *never* know. Every time I was outside, I began to look up at the sky. My teenagers asked me one day, "What are you doing?"

I explained to them what I had asked God for. They all thought I was really losing it! A couple of times I thought I had seen cross-shaped clouds, but it was just jet fumes! Then finally, after weeks of watching for my cross clouds, I was driving down a familiar hill to town and sure enough, right in front of me was a huge cross cloud! And it wasn't jet fumes either! I knew it was MY cross cloud! God loves me!

When I got home, I told the kids. They all looked at each other again with the same look—"She is really a crazy woman!" I could tell that they did not believe me. I began to pray, "Lord, the next time You give me a cross cloud, please let my kids see it too."

Again weeks passed. Then one day we were driving to church to prepare for my parents' fiftieth wedding anniversary. I had been working hard on the preparations for a few months, and the next day was to be the celebration. My oldest daughter Hannah was driving, and as we were traveling toward the church, she pointed out the window and said, "Look, Mom!"

On our left up in the sky was a beautiful cross-shaped cloud! They ALL saw it. I knew that God was saying to me, "I love you. I like what you are doing for your parents. I am pleased that you are doing this for them."

Can you believe it? I knew it was God, and I knew He loved me—me!

– Patty Albert

4

I prayed for a new dress for Christmas, but as I looked, all of the ones I liked were over—way over—my budget. I asked God for a brand new dress—not a thrift-store special. So I started saving money. As time went on, I put every extra penny in a bank account along with all money gifts other than tithes.

In the meantime I fell twice and hurt my knees. I went to my regular doctor, and she said I needed to go to an orthopedic doctor. I knew that would be a strain on our finances, so I prayed for God to heal me, but that wasn't His plan. I said, "Okay, Lord, I trust You, but what am I going to do? I can't work."

Well, I decided to see how much money I had hidden away in the bank. I couldn't believe it—$500! So I prayed for an orthopedic doctor, and God gave me Dr. Quinlan, a Christian. He x-rayed, examined, and gave me a cortisone shot. I said, "How much is my bill (thinking $500)?"

He said, "No charge."

The following Monday I went on a ladies' shopping fellowship, and there was a 70% off clearance rack. I bought **four** brand-new suits for $80! God loves me!

– Cheryl Crews

I feel very loved by the Lord when I see an eastern bluebird. These lovely little creatures are a brilliant blue with a robin-like breast. Of course, the male is the brightest, most beautiful one!

I have two bluebird houses in my yard. Typically they raise two to three families each summer with four or five babies in each family. These little birds don't mind if you open the birdhouse and look at the eggs/babies. I get to enjoy them as they fly around, and then I get a close-up in the nest.

The Lord gave me a special blessing this past spring when a bluebird family built a nest in the mailbox post in front of my office at the church. Almost daily I watched the parents go in and out of that makeshift house.

I have information from a man who builds bluebird houses which says that the babies stay in the nest for 17 days after they hatch. The parents feverishly bring them food for those 17 days. What a blessing to watch them take care of their little ones.

Since these little birds are territorial, I get to enjoy them all the time. They actually winter-over in our area in the bluebird house! I feel so loved by God year round!

– Renee Cox

6

I do not have a specific bird or animal or item of some sort that reminds me of God's love when I see it. I know God loves me because He saved my soul and has answered so many prayers. But I know God REALLY loves me, and I feel a special love when He answers a prayer that I know I am the only one who is praying, AND it is something really insignificant and totally female! The following is a prime example. I was so astounded at the sequence of events.

Several months ago I lost a favorite earring. It was not just any old ordinary earring. I had purchased it from one of our ladies who sells Premiere Design, so it was not inexpensive. It had a pearl (not real) in the middle, and tiny, very sparkly crystals surrounded the pearl. (I love sparkle!) But that's not all. They were CLIP earrings. I am a die-hard clip earring wearer, and they are not always easy to find. I have never thought it to be a good idea to poke holes in myself. Truth is, I have a very weak stomach when it comes to things like that. Well, anyway, I lost one. I prayed. Several weeks passed, and I could not locate that earring.

Every month or more I meet with seven ladies, and we plan the church socials and banquets. At this particular meeting, Georgia Camp was telling about an answer to prayer that she had. I jokingly told her that I should have her pray for my ear-ring since I had not gotten an answer yet. I described in great detail what the earring looked like, and much to my amaze-ment, she said that her daughter Samantha had found some-thing that looked like that but thought it was a pendant that you put on a chain to wear around your neck. I guess they had never seen a clip earring up close before. Does that beat all?? Georgia promised to bring it to church on Sunday.

Would you believe? It was my earring! Do you know where they found it? In one of those expansion cracks in the driveway that goes by the church dumpster! Apparently I had made a trip to the dumpster, and in the process, the earring had fallen off. I can't begin to tell you how many cars had driven over that crack in a three-week period, but it was still in perfect condi-tion. It must have been just far enough down in the crack or expansion joint that it was protected. God had protected that earring, the sparkle had caught the eye of one of our teenage girls, and my earring was found.

Do I feel loved? YOU BET I DO!!!!!

– Betty Morrow

7

After the 2006 ladies' Spectacular in Durham, North Carolina, I was driving home all alone and meditating over the godly instruction, encouragement, excitement, and blessings that occurred over the course of the Spectacular. As I thought on what I had heard, one thing stuck out to me, and that was what Mrs. Schaap had said about God's being real to you and the ways He has shown you He loves you. I thought on this and began to cry because I thought about how God did love me and all of the wonderful things He has done for me.

After praising God and crying, I asked God to show me one thing in particular, like Mrs. Schaap has done, to remind me how much He loves me. It was raining that Saturday, and the sun was beginning to show its face when I told the Lord how nice it would be to see a rainbow and how that could be a way He could show me He loved me and let me know He was really hearing my praises to Him.

No sooner had I said this when out of my driver's side window over my left shoulder did I see a huge, beautiful rainbow that seemed like it couldn't get any closer to me. I wept so much that I thought I would have to pull over to even keep driving. I will never forget that day, Lord willing, for as long as I live. Each time since when I see a rainbow in the sky or on any type of object, I am reminded that God loves me!

P. S. I thought it was special that a rainbow is one of God's promises too! (Genesis 9:13)

– Monica Gunter

As Brother Golia begins dismissing Sunday school classes, excitement builds up inside me. Once again, it is the highlight of my week—the time that is spent helping to change lives. It is the time when I get the privilege of standing before my third and fourth grade bus girls and sharing with them how much God and I love each one of them and how God has a special plan for each of their lives.

I can see each of my girls begin to squirm with anticipation as our turn to be dismissed approaches. As our class is dismissed, each girl files into an almost perfectly straight line behind me, and we quietly walk to our classroom. Cheerfully, I greet my girls, "Good morning, ladies!"

"Good morning, Miss Ruby!" comes the echoing reply.

As I look into each face, my eyes pause for a brief moment on the face of a young girl who rides my bus. I can see the pain masked by the joy of being in this haven of rest. Since I have the opportunity to visit this young girl's home every week, I am aware of the many struggles through which her family goes—everything from abuse to living in a broken, dirty house. It breaks my heart every time to think what these girls go through.

I bring my attention back to the present and begin the lesson. This week's lesson stresses how each person is special to God and how He loves each individual in a special way. I challenge each of my girls to choose a "God loves me" sign—something that will remind her of God's unconditional love.

One girl raises her hand and asks rather timidly, "Miss Ruby, how do you know God loves you?"

"Well," I reply, "when I lived at home with my mom, I used to go into the woods when I wanted to be alone. I would often sit and watch wild animals. Sometimes I would see deer. Once I even saw a moose!" Mouths drop open, and eyes grow big. I realize that the only "wildlife" most of these girls have ever seen are the squirrels that roam Chicago.

I softly chuckle to myself and continue with my story. "Since I came to college, I rarely see deer anymore. One day I told God that I was going to make deer my sign."

Up came several hands. One girl asks, "Miss Ruby, does God really let you see real, live deer?"

I smile and tell them, "Yes, God really does let me see real, live deer." I also explain that I have not seen deer in quite a while, but God still loves me even when I don't see deer."

After class the young girl who rides my bus walks up and wraps her arms tightly around me. "Miss Ruby," she says barely above a whisper, "I know God loves me when I see you."

Tears threaten to spill down my face as, in a choked voice, I inquire as to the reason she has chosen me to be her "God loves me" sign.

"Because then I know God loves me every week," is the somewhat muffled reply.

Some may think that faithfulness is not really that important, but they don't realize that one week can make a difference. Who will never know that God loves them simply because you only missed one week?

– Ruby Barnes

9

I know God loves me when my husband reaches over and takes my hand while we are walking together. I feel the earthly touch of the Heavenly Father, and I know He holds my hand!

– Helen MacCormack

10

Every time my baby cries, God shows me He loves me! After a stillbirth and several miscarriages, the Lord blessed my husband and me with a handsome baby boy on December 29, 2006. I would pray every day while I was pregnant that the Lord would just allow me to hear my baby cry. Now when he cries, that is my reminder of how much God loves me for being faithful and trusting Him.

– Chastity Mott

11

I feel like God is saying, "I love you, Melinda" when I really need a new skirt and He helps me find a really good bargain at the store. The other day He sent me ten new skirts from a stranger. Every one of them fit perfectly. Isn't God good to His children? I'm so glad I belong to Him.

– Melinda Gibbs

12

The date was April 20, 2007; it was our middle son's birthday. He would have been 50 years old—but for the last almost ten years now, Kevin has been in Heaven. My husband also went to Heaven almost three years ago—so there I was alone with my memories on this special day. Remembering—so many precious memories.

My sweet and caring daughter-in-law, Kevin's widow, called me, and we shared sweet memories as we do on every special day—birthdays, anniversaries, the day they went Home to Heaven, etc.

But then came this unexpected call from a friend at my church—a young wife and mother of two little ones. She was calling to tell me she loved me so much—like a grandma. She said she was so grateful for my mentoring her as a young wife and mother according to God's Word. She did not know it was Kevin's birthday, but God knew, and I suddenly felt so loved by my Father in Heaven! He knew I needed this "hug" from Him!

– Mary Rabe

13

Once as our pastor, Dr. Jack Schaap, preached about choosing something that reminds you how much God loves you, I began to think about what I would choose. During a rainstorm, it hit me—lightning (not literally, of course!). Why lightning? Well, there is something amazing about the dazzling light and the amount of power wielded in that streak of lightning. It's quite beautiful as well as terrifying. Most people, including me, have a healthy fear of it.

Likewise, I have a healthy fear of the Lord. I am in awe of Him; I am dazzled by Him, and I respect the power that He wields. It gave a better understanding of Proverbs 1:7a, "*The fear of the LORD is the beginning of knowledge....*" That explanation leads me to my story.

One July I was able to surprise my husband with a mini-getaway. Just the two of us had not had a vacation together in a long time, and he was long overdue for one. Of course, money was tight, but I prayed for God to give me wisdom about how to go about this. I was able to secure a fantastic rate at a four-star hotel for three days and two nights in Chicago. I called my cousin about valet parking, and he was able to get us free parking—another savings of $27 per night! When we got to our room on the eighteenth floor, I looked out over the gloomy, yet beautiful, Chicago skyline. I whispered a prayer of thanks to God for all that went into this trip with the little money I had.

Just as I finished my prayer, a tiny streak of lightning flashed in the distance. It was like God was telling me, "You're welcome! I did it because I love you."

I felt like I would burst. I turned to my husband and told him about the whole lightning idea (I hadn't told anyone up to that point) and how God "answered" me when I thanked Him. We laughed, and he teased me about how I chose something that could potentially hurt others.

That evening my cousin surprised us with a car and a driver to take us to the restaurant of our choice, on him. What a pleasant evening! No worries about traffic or parking and a wonderful meal at a steakhouse. I couldn't have asked for more. When we returned, my husband hugged me and said, "God must love you a whole lot."

I said, "Yes, He does. I don't understand, but sometimes I feel like I'm one of His favorites." (By the way, I think He makes everyone feel uniquely special.) That night God put on a spectacular lightning show that was breathtaking.

I always say that when I die, there will be a beautiful lightning show to let people know that I am basking in His love.

– Olga Vega

14

About six months ago, the Lord inspired me through reading an article in the *Christian Womanhood* magazine. For several years I could not understand the significance or the blessing of having something that says "I love you" from the Lord. I had not given it much consideration. After reading the article, I knew I wanted to have similar experiences. I am not sure exactly why, but I chose a rare native New Zealand bird called a "fantail." They are small and fly in the same manner as a hummingbird. When they are flying, their tail is not spread, but as soon as they land, it immediately opens to a beautiful fan; hence, their name "fantails." I had only seen them maybe two to three times in the almost eleven years that we've lived in New Zealand, but I immediately became intrigued by them.

I found myself looking for His "I love you"s all the time. One morning our son Matthew ran into the room exclaiming that I had to come and see something. What he showed me was amazing—we had not one, but two fantails living in our orchard in the back section of our property! A few days later he snapped an amazing photograph, truly amazing because it is hard to catch them still for very long.

I'm not actually sure if they were residents or just visiting because I only saw them again twice. One of those times was an experience I'll never forget. For some reason, I was incredibly homesick. After ten years on the mission field, homesickness is not usually accompanied by tears, but I was crying buckets. I ached to be with my family members—to hug them—to laugh with them—just to sit in the same room with them. I was sitting on the bed and cried, "Lord, please just tell me once again that You want us here. I need Your love."

Immediately, three fantails landed on the tree right outside my window. I was stunned, thrilled, awed, overjoyed, and even more emotional as I almost physically felt the sweet arms of Jesus around me.

Thank you, Mrs. Schaap. If it had not been for your article, I might have missed the whole experience.

– Amber Bosje

15

I am an assistant Sunday school teacher in our two- and three-year-olds class, as well as a bus worker. Sometimes I've had a very hard week and feel like "throwing in the towel." Right when I walk in the classroom and feel like quitting, God sends one of those little ones to hug me and say, "I love you, Miss Michelle!" It makes it all worth it—especially when one of the bus kids trusts Christ.

– Michelle Lonaberger

16

My pastor-husband and I were praying and praying for a bigger church building since our present building was small and getting crowded. My husband began looking for a building, but everything cost in the millions. Obviously, we couldn't afford any of them. We put up our church building for sale, prayed, and waited. A new building seemed like an impossibility.

One day a pastor from a nearby church called my husband and told him he was resigning and wanted him to take over his church building. We were excited! Our church members were excited too! The new church building, worth $1.8 million, had just been remodeled and was completely debt-free. Needless to say, we all jumped at the offer. Yes, my husband and I both felt very loved by God, and so did our church members.

– Peedy Hertzel

17

The week of our church's Christmas banquet, I naturally was thinking of what to wear. I thought to myself, "How nice it would be to have a snowflake necklace to go with my snowflake earrings."

When I went to church that week, a couple who are not members but had been visiting our church came just to give me a gift. When the husband handed me the gift, he explained that they could not stay because his wife was not feeling well, but she had wanted to give me something. "Open it later," were his parting words.

I took my children to their classes, and then I opened the gift. I'm sure you already know what it was—a snowflake necklace—the most beautiful one I have ever seen! Right away I thanked God for the necklace. But then I read her note, and this is when I began to cry. She wrote, "God told me to buy this for you, Linda. But then I had to ask Him for your last name because I know so many Lindas. He told me Linda Crabb."

She then wrote how she told God, "But I don't know her very well—she might not accept it from me."

God then told her to tell me it was from Him.

I was just amazed that God would do that for me, one who is so unworthy. I also thought how many times we pass up blessings because we can't believe God would want to do something like that for someone through us. This dear lady was so thankful that God would use her to buy it for me.

Then I thought how God blesses us all the time, and we don't acknowledge it—like our health, children, husband, friends, and being used to lead people to Christ or help others. My beautiful snowflake necklace will always remind me of God's blessings.   – Linda Crabb

18

When I was a young girl, I dreamed of having a family of my own. Growing up, I had many health problems. I remember like it was yesterday when the doctors told my mom that I might not be able to carry a child. I was only 15, but my heart was broken. I never told anyone, and my mom was the only one who knew what the doctors had said. As time passed, I understood how important it was to most men to have a son or a daughter to call their own. I would hear sermons on the importance of family. When I heard the announcements in church of a new arrival, I would silently think, "Who is going to marry someone who can't give them a child?" It would be one thing to marry and not know that you were unable to have children, but I would have to tell the person eventually that the dream of having a child was not possible with me.

Well, God gave me not just a husband, but the greatest man in the whole world. In 2004 God blessed me with a surprise—I discovered I was expecting. Numerous times I was in the hospital. Numerous times I was told that I would have a miscarriage. Numerous times a week I would meet with the team of doctors who were going to deliver my child. Numerous times I shed tears while I suffered pain five, six, seven, and eight months too early. On January 13, 2005, Benjamin Francisco Stephens came into our lives—one month early. Although he was in the intensive care unit for ten days, he came home and has been the light of my life every day.

I think back to the day the doctor told my mom I would not be able to carry a child. Then I smile as my son runs around, and I think, "I couldn't carry a child, but God could." I'm now in nursing school, and if there is one thing I have learned from professors, it is that medical science has its limitations, and doctors make human errors. However, God has no limitations and makes no errors.

When my husband and my son smile at me, it's as if God Himself whispers in my ear, "I love you."

–Maricela Stephens

19

Over the past couple of years, I have had some health issues. God has given me grace and shown me that He truly loves me at the time I seem to need it most by other's encouraging me and praying for me. Also hearing encouragement from Mrs. JoJo Moffitt and Mrs. Marlene Evans over the years has been a true blessing.   – Angie West

20

In 2005 I was just coming out the other side of some major storms and trials in my life. My two boys were both ready to start school all day, and I wanted desperately to invest what little time and talent I had for the Lord. I told God and my husband what a dream it would be to have the opportunity to work with women like Mrs. Schaap at Christian Womanhood. I never told another soul my heart's desire.

I had allowed the Devil to make me believe that God did not love me and that I was unusable. Why should I even ask for something so unattainable? I decided to fervently pray and dubbed it "my ceiling talks." Every day I would cry, beg, plead, and ask God to show me He loved me and that He was real. For six months I did this without fail.

One August day I was completely spent and ready to give up. I was tired of praying and God's not answering in **my** time. (I must admit my heart is always convicted by Psalm 27:14, *"Wait on the LORD: be of good courage, and he shall strengthen thine heart: wait, I say, on the LORD."* I wish I could hurry up and have patience NOW!)

That day I received a call from Christian Womanhood. Out of what seemed like nowhere, I was asked to be Jane Grafton's Spectacular assistant. [The Spectacular is an international ladies' conference hosted by First Baptist Church of Hammond, Indiana, every October.] This was a temporary seven-week job that turned into a permanent part-time position with Christian Womanhood as the marketing director. This job opportunity may seem to some as just that—a wonderful job opportunity. But to me, it is God's reaching down and showing me His love in a very wonderfully specific way. Every single time I walk from my car to the Christian Womanhood office, I thank God for His love to me. What a loving Father we serve!

– Julie Busby

21

I am a Hyles-Anderson College student from the state of Pennsylvania. I love my home state, so every time I see a Pennsylvania license plate or place a call to Pennsylvania from my workplace, I am reminded that God loves me.

– Jamie Beaverson

22

When I lost my son in March 2005, I felt overwhelmed. Everything was happening so fast—making arrangements to go to the hospital and for supervision of my other two children—I felt God was keeping my mind busy. I came home from the hospital on a Friday evening, and the grand opening of our new church building at First Baptist Church of Hammond, Indiana, was the following Sunday. I felt there was no way I could attend the service. I couldn't face the reminders with all of the "I'm sorrys." I wanted to close my mind, try to forget, and move on. Still, I felt compelled that Saturday night to go ahead and attend church the next day.

Little did I know that God would fill a need that Sunday morning that I never knew was possible. Pastor Schaap preached a sermon entitled, "Glory From the Graves." I knew God was using Brother Schaap to reach me that day. Although I had just lost my son and felt that my earthly world was caving in on me, God told me it would be all right. His grace surrounded me that afternoon, and although I will never fully understand God's purpose in the loss of my son, I know God loves me more than I loved my son, and I'm okay with that. God comforted me at a time when I wasn't sure I could be comforted, and that is how God showed me that He loves me.

– Amanda Huckins

23

*S*ometime before my first husband passed away, I prayed the prayer of Jabez after hearing a special speaker who had come to our church in Sawyer, Michigan. When he passed away after many years of illness, I prayed the following prayer on my knees in front of my special place—my yellow velvet chair:

1. Lord, if You have anyone for me, let it be the first one who asks me for a date.
2. Let him be the very best for me.
3. Have him go out of his way to see me.

I really did forget all about the prayer until later because I was exhausted from working many hours.

One Saturday the phone rang, and someone said, "How would you like to go out to dinner tonight?"

"Who is this?" I asked.

"Casey Vinke," he replied. "I shook your hand New Year's Eve at church."

We went to a nice restaurant in St. Joseph, Michigan. All at once it seemed the Lord and I were the only ones there. "Lord," I said, "this is someone special."

We were married shortly after. Casey said the preacher pointed me out to him. His first wife, daughter, and a niece had been tragically killed in an automobile accident in 1973. Thirty-two years later we both know God never makes a mistake!   – Millie Vinke

24

I love watching birds in my yard. God has been very good to me—several different, interesting, and beautiful birds come for birdseed and suet. My favorites are hummingbirds. This year I put up a sugar water feeder in my backyard on March 15—the date a friend uses who gets them to come to her feeders every year. I watched in vain and kept telling the Lord how much I wanted to see them in my yard.

One morning in July when I was feeling a little down and really needed to be reminded that God loves me, I pulled up my blinds on a window in the front of the house and saw a hummingbird darting in and out of gladioli blossoms in my front yard. The next morning I got a bonus from the Lord. As I pulled up the blinds, I thought to myself, "This is about the same time of morning that I did this yesterday," looked out, and there he was again!   – Yvonne Coats

25

I have been in and out of the penitentiary all of my adult life (six times for selling drugs). God has showed His love in my life through the change that has occurred since I trusted Christ and joined First Baptist Church of Hammond. I'm clean and sober since being baptized here on April 1, 2006. I have also joined John McCollam's Sunday school class.

                                                        – Derrick Brooks

26

I had been on drugs and alcohol and into prostitution most of my life. Since I trusted Christ and joined First Baptist Church of Hammond, God has revealed His love to me by helping me to stay clean and sober for nine months.　　– Felicia Anderson

27

I had a severe stroke, and doctors told me I wouldn't make it. But God brought me through.　　　　　　　　– Bonnie Brock

28

My story may be similar to others in that I use pennies as a reminder that God loves me. I'm 22, almost 23, and since my freshman year of high school, pennies have been particularly special to me. It started when I would find one, put it in my shoe, and "make a wish." I shared this with my friend, now my husband Dan, and he started doing it too. When the penny would move in his shoe, it reminded him to think of me. We are still doing this. Almost every time I found a penny, I would correlate that special coin as a specific and personal way that God was telling me that He loves me.

I don't always put the pennies I find in my shoe now, but I often find them by my car door or on sidewalks and curbs—just everywhere. I always get so thrilled, not that the news of God's love is new to me, but how He would take His precious "time" to tell me often how much He loves me in such a pointed way.

– Stacy Harrell

29

 know God loves me because He led me here to First Baptist Church of Hammond, Indiana. He put a roof over my head, and He helped me get a job. Even though I felt at times He was not with me, I know He has been and will continue to be.

– Therasa Phillips

30

 n high school I started collecting coins and postage stamps. Instead of hunting for or purchasing them, I allow God to send them to me.

Sometimes mail comes with pretty stamps that somehow missed being canceled at the post office. I smile really big and say, "Ooooh, look God! Thanks!" I know God just sent me an "I love you," and it goes in my album.

It's the same with coins. I find them in parking lots, in stores, in change people give to me, and when I find a wheat cent, I get really excited. I know God is letting me know He loves me. Once He even gave me a penny from the 1890s!

Now my children have caught on, and when they find a

penny (which is quite often), they yell out, "Mama! Look what I found! Jesus loves me!"

Then I smile and my heart swells with joy, and I say, "Yes, He does."   – Julie Macewicz

31

The best way I know God loves me is that the Bible says in John 3:16, *"For God so loved the world, that he gave his only begotten Son, that whosoever believeth in him should not perish, but have everlasting life."* Jesus loves me so much He stretched out His arms and died.

I am often reminded of God's love, but I want to also remind Him that I love Him. When I see a penny, I tell God I love Him. I have found many pennies—as well as dimes, nickels, and quarters!   – Cheri Genske

32

In 1993 after I had tried ten or fifteen different churches, a bus worker on Charlie Fryermuth's bus route from Marion Avenue Baptist Church in Washington, Iowa, knocked on my family's apartment door. I started going to church on a bus. At this church I learned that God loves me.

God showed me He loved me that day by sending someone to show me the path to Him.

– Christina Sears

33

My daughter Kalynn went to Hyles-Anderson College and graduated in 2007. While she was in school, I prayed every day that she would do God's will. I said, "Lord, it sure would be nice if she was hired by our own home church so that she could be around women who would be a good influence on her life." I also prayed that she would get hired before she graduated. God answered all three of those prayers.

I am reminded of God's love when I have the privilege of watching her be a part of the Christian Womanhood staff. I am very proud of Kalynn, and I think I have the greatest daughter a mom could want.

– Darlene Suba

34

The way I am reminded that God loves me is by getting front row parking spaces. One day I was driving down the row and saw the fourth spot open, but then a car cut me off and parked there. I jokingly said, "Okay, God. I guess You don't love me very much!" Then as I drove down a little farther, the very first spot was open! I started laughing, told God He has a great sense of humor, and I felt very loved by Him.

– Priscilla Duff

35

Our family decided that when we saw deer, God was showing us He loved us. One day after my children came out of school, we were driving home. I was very upset, and we were kind of disagreeing and arguing. I started to turn left when my son Ruben excitedly screamed for us to turn the other way because he had seen two deer! All of us stood quietly and watched them. This moment was so great because we felt God's love. We even forgot what we had just been arguing about! We went home and had a sweet, peaceful dinner!

– Gina Paredes

36

God shows me He loves me by answering my questions. I love feeling like I have a delicious secret—I can ask God, the Creator of the universe, a question, and He answers me. Just recently I was struggling with an area of faith. I told God the honest truths that were in my cold heart regarding a certain subject. I asked Him to give me His perspective. Within a week I read a Bible passage and heard a sermon that directly and unequivocally answered the question I had posed to God.

He loves me. He answers all my questions, and my spirit soars within me whenever that happens.

– Patricia White

37

I was very happily married at the age of 19. My husband and I had always been very happy together as we had spent a lot of time together getting to know each other before we married. Several months went by, and my husband had talked me into moving to Puerto Rico with him. That is where he was from, so that is what we did. I loved it quickly because it is so very beautiful. We already had a daughter, and soon I was expecting my second born—my son. Not long after moving to Puerto Rico, my husband became an entirely new person. The one who had made sure I did not smoke or drink was all of a sudden partying, drinking, out with women, and no longer saw me as the best friend or as the wife for whom he once had so many feelings.

He told me to divorce him and go back home. I did not believe in divorce, and so I did everything in my power to save my marriage. I refused to leave, and I refused to sign for a divorce. I tried to be the wife he wanted and tried to make him happy, but he had already made up his mind. Because I was expecting at this time, it was a very stressful time for me to say the least. We went on with his trying to get me to leave and my trying to save the marriage.

After the delivery of my son, he would take the kids to show them to his girlfriend. All this, and I still kept hope alive. He was a very determined man, and just a couple of months after the birth of my son, he became abusive. I no longer was wanted in his life, and he was going to find a way to make me leave.

Needless to say, he won. I was young, had fought a long, hard fight, and knew nothing more to do but leave and go back home. I hesitantly signed the papers, and we were divorced. I had walked out of a marriage because I felt I had no other choice; it was over. (He has since passed away from a motorcycle accident.)

One month later I was back home temporarily living with my parents while working and trying to support my two children. I found myself in a new chapter of my life as a single mom. Because of all I had been through, I told myself, "If that is what marriage is all about, I want no part of it." I did not want to remarry. Life became a bit depressing, but my kids kept me going. I had gotten an apartment for the kids and me, worked a job to make a living, and life was okay.

As time went on, I got behind on bills; it was not an easy job being a single parent. I was having a hard time. Out of the blue, my sister, who lived in Kansas, called. She was able to see that I was having a hard time, and during our conversation she mentioned "a nice guy" who had been praying that God would send him a wife.

Well, I was not interested! I had two kids. Who on earth wants to marry someone who already has children? I felt doomed to being single forever.

Still, this "nice guy" called me a week later. I, not being interested, graciously "blew him off." For some reason he called again within a couple of weeks. I thought I should let him talk a bit, and so we did—no big deal—just small talk. Well, that small talk was the start of having a nice friend with whom to talk now and then, right into a very good long-distance friend of whom I had never even seen a picture. We continued our over-the-phone relationship.

Shortly after I began talking to this gentleman, my sister planned to come home for a two-week visit. I was very excited as I had not seen her in quite a long time. She flew home, and I picked her up at the airport. At the time I had been wrongly fired from my job, my home church had burned to the ground, and I was told to catch up on my back rent or move out within two weeks. It was no coincidence that all of this happened the way it did.

My sister had been telling me that I should move to Kansas with her, and she decided to tear up her plane ticket and told me, "Now you can drive me home."

Feeling like my world was collapsing around me, I packed up everything that would fit in my little car, got rid of the rest, and in two weeks, I found myself on my way to Kansas. I was excited and nervous, not knowing what to expect.

I knew inside of myself that the "nice guy" in Kansas was really nice, and I knew that I liked what I knew about him. When I arrived in Kansas, the "nice guy" met me with a very beautiful bouquet of flowers and graciously welcomed me. We were finally able to meet each other face to face.

He shared with me how he had been sent to Kansas to an Army base and how he thought it was all a mistake because he was in the Air Force and did not want to go to Kansas. Some soul winners from a local Baptist church put a tract in his door, and he decided to visit the church. That is how he met my sister and brother-in-law. He told me that he had been praying God would send him a wife, and all of a sudden, there I was.

We spent the next several months getting to know each other. Over time we really felt that God had indeed brought us together. He asked me to marry him, and needless to say, I could not resist. It was the beginning of what I call a second chance.

I feel so loved by God to have been given a second chance in marriage. We have now been married for 15 wonderful years. We have three more children, and my older two were taken in by this man who loves them to death and has always done for them as if they were his own. I cannot even begin to tell you how blessed I feel. I am married to the most wonderful man— the man of my dreams. We have become best friends and have what we call the *best* marriage. So that is my story of how God loved me so much that He gave me a second chance in marriage, and for that I will be forever thankful.

– Lori Flores

My special way that God tells me that He loves me is when it is a cloudy day and the sun just peeks through the clouds and sends downs rays of sunshine that you can see. It is then that I say, "I love You too, Jesus."

When my dad was dying, he requested that I sing the song "Daddy's Hands" for his funeral. I had tried to get the sheet music and found out that it would take two weeks to get it, and I only had three days. I went to the local Christian bookstore and looked there for the music. Every song was supposed to be in alphabetical order, so I looked through the "Ds," and it was not there. I kept looking through the music, and alphabetized with the "Qs," with the cover facing up, was a tape case with a picture of the sun breaking through the clouds. The rays of sunshine were falling upon the words of the song—"Daddy's Hands." Right there in the store, I said out loud, "I love You too, Jesus!" I received some strange looks, but I knew what my Saviour had done, and He wanted me to know it too.

I took the song to my dad, and he said, "Did you get the tape made?" (I knew I wouldn't be able to sing the song at the funeral, so I recorded my singing it.) I said, "Yes," and he said, "Let me hear it."

I put in the tape, and we listened together to the song that meant so much to him. My dad went to Heaven the next day with a smile on his face. God is so good.

– Vickie Atchinson

39

My reminder or "sign" from God that He loves me is black and white butterflies. When Ricky and I first arrived as missionaries in the Philippines, I hardly ever saw butterflies around our property. I had heard Mrs. Cindy Schaap's talk about God showing us He loves us and searching for the reminders He sends, so I began to pray that He would send a black and white butterfly.

A few Sundays later while sitting in church on a Sunday morning, a huge black and white butterfly flew right across the chapel, and not only that, but it almost flew right into my face! I grabbed my mother-in-law's arm and said, "God loves ME!!"

We later took a trip to the north side of our island and visited a butterfly farm! My husband took some gorgeous pictures of the black and white butterflies, and we had them enlarged and framed. I had the honor of teaching English to the second year ladies of our Bible college. I used Mrs. Schaap's lesson and my experiences in a lesson to the girls. I had them pray and choose something to remind them that God is crazy about them! It was a blessing to me as different girls wrote to me (some using paper with butterflies on it) and told me about how God shows that He loves them. One girl even chose a cockroach!

Thank you, Mrs. Schaap, for your lesson and for helping people all over the world realize God truly is crazy about His children.   – Brandie Martin

40

When I was in college, Mrs. Marlene Evans encouraged our class to pick something special to us. Whenever we saw something special, it would remind us of God's love for us—a kind of hug from Him. I chose cardinals and rainbows.

Over the last seven years, God has allowed my family to go through some difficult valleys. In 2000 my husband left, and I was the single mother of three young boys. Little did I know this was the first of several valleys through which He would lead me. In the winter of 2003, Christmas Day to be exact, my son

Dakota became violently ill. He was screaming and pulling out his hair. He soon went blind in his left eye and lost partial vision in his right eye. I took him to the eye doctor, only to be told he would need a CT scan. Two hours after he had the scan, the doctor called to tell me that my son had three tumors. An MRI soon determined that it was a tumor the size of a tennis ball. I was told he had to have surgery.

On February 17, 2004, the surgeon removed a tumor the size of a baseball. He was surprised at the size since it appeared smaller in the MRI. My son is doing fine with only a small piece of the tumor remaining. During this difficult time, I saw an amazing sight in the middle of winter—a rainbow going from cloud to cloud. I was reminded of God's love.

My son Dustin has severe asthma. He was in and out of the hospital for three years before the medical world figured out the cause. The problem was fixed, and he is fine. In the hospital each time I saw a rainbow on the wall colored by a little girl with cystic fibrosis, I was reminded of God's love.

My youngest son Donovan has a form of autism known as Aspberger's Syndrome. For the past three years, I have seen several cardinals at specific times. On two occasions, when Donovan had had a rough day and I was at the end of my rope, I saw a cardinal on my back porch. Each time I was reminded of God's love.

In May of this year, I was diagnosed with cancer. My friend, Andy Sontag, heard of my story of how cardinals were a way I saw God's love for me. He liked the story but reminded me that God's love was not random. It is an ever-present love that is all encompassing. He gave me a figurine of a cardinal to set on my night stand and one to hang in my room. These were to remind me every day of God's love for me.

Every one of us knows that God loves us. And every once in a while, we may wish that God would reach down and give us a big hug. Every morning I get to wake up and see the cardinals in my room. Seeing them is the hug I need to get through the day. Choose something that is special to you and get your hugs from God!   – Kristina Alexander

#1

God gifted me with a wonderful husband Tom and then two children, Lee and Madison. On Wednesday, November 16, 2006, a day of which I have no memory, I was driving Lee, Madison, and a friend of Lee's home. It had been snowing for a couple of hours, and there was a heavy coating of snow on the road. I suddenly lost control of the van and slid into the lane of an oncoming, empty propane tanker truck. The truck driver was not injured; but shortly after the impact, God called our children and their friend Michael to Heaven.

I was critically injured and was kept heavily sedated for several days while doctors attended to my healing in the critical care unit of Spectrum Butterworth Hospital in Grand Rapids, Michigan. My main injuries consisted of fractured C5 & C6 neck vertebra; a shattered right femur (thigh bone); a non-traditional stroke with paralysis on my right side, especially the right hand and arm; additional brain swelling and damage from the impact; a baseball-size hole in my diaphragm; and smaller fractures. I was on a respirator for a while and had a feeding tube in my stomach. I was unable to speak because of the tracheotomy.

Unsure of the extent of my brain damage, the doctors told Tom that I had to ask about the kids. No one was to volunteer the information that they were gone. Soon after awakening (coincidentally the day of the funeral), I mouthed the question asking where the kids were.

I was in the medical hospital for two weeks and the rehab hospital for two more weeks. I came home on December 16. Healing comes in steps—getting off the ventilator; learning how to walk and do basic personal care with a 12-pound halo on my head to hold my neck straight, a weakened right side, a broken leg held together by a rod and pins, and blurred vision. Dealing with a tracheotomy made speaking impossible at first. The paralysis affected my ability to swallow and eat solid foods. Then came intense physical, occupational, speech, and grief therapy; and the removal of the halo. I distinctly remember January 20, after my halo was removed, how great it felt to take a shower without all the heavy, wet fleece and the mechanics on my torso, and to know that Tom didn't have to take two hours changing them. Each of these healing steps was a vivid reminder to me of God's love.

No one but God can be credited for quickly healing my body and, bit by bit, our hearts after such an unimaginable, devastating experience. He loved us through it all, went before us, and was there to lift us out of the pit of human despair. The outpouring of love, care, and help we received from family, friends, and our community was incredible! I was especially touched by the demonstration of love and care from people we did not even know.

We journaled our journey through this difficult time, and one day my husband wrote, "A friend of ours said that now we are our children's heritage; we carry on what they have started. I hope and pray that I will be able to live up to them in a very special and honorable way."

God brought and continues to bring wonderful people into our lives. He has led us to a beautiful blend of traditional and alternative healers, allowing me to be off ALL pain and medication just two weeks after the accident; people to comfort us; and those we are helping to comfort. Lee and Madison, our children, continue to bring people to Christ—completing the circle for eternal life.

Over time sad, distraught thoughts are being replaced with comforting memories. God's grace and mercy get total credit. God had led beautiful and wonderful people into the lives of our children, touching their lives in more ways than we could know. Even though we are comforted, we still get "sucker-punched" unexpectedly with thoughts of what will never be in their earthly lives. So we cry through it and remain grateful for all the fun and blessings we had together, blessings of which so many others are robbed—sometimes by early death and sometimes from emotional distance and physical neglect.

Ironically, as a licensed funeral director, I was unable to attend the funerals of our children as I was still in the critical care unit. We decided when I was physically able, we would have a memorial service for Lee and Maddie. We did have a wonderfully sweet service for them on June 3, 2006…another step of the healing process. Through it all, God has shown His love to me in ways too numerous to count. If God didn't love me, my world would be in shambles, without hope or love. God is good, and He loves me!   – Marie Bennett

42

*I*t was summertime, and our city was in the middle of quite a serious drought. Water restrictions were being heavily imposed upon our city—no washing cars, no watering lawns, etc. I was at my breakfast table one morning reading my *Christian Womanhood* magazine. I was reading Mrs. Cindy Schaap's editor's notes telling how she is reminded God loves her every time she sees a hummingbird, and that her daughter is reminded of God's love every time she sees blue skies with no clouds. I had read before about ways others are reminded that God loves them, and I said, "Lord, I need a special way for You to show Your love for me too."

No sooner had I said that, than little drops of water started hitting the skylight right above my head. I thought to myself, "Lord, You have got to be kidding me! Are You serious—rain? Great! That figures! Other people have butterflies, deer, pennies, blue skies, and hummingbirds. Not me; I get rain."

At first, I have to admit, I was a little offended. I was embarrassed to tell anyone how I was reminded that God loved me. Nevertheless, every time it would rain I would tell the Lord, "I know You love me, and I love You too. Thank You, Lord, for the rain." Something happened in my heart! You know what? I began to love the rain! I would look forward to the rain!

We didn't get a lot of rain, and I would find myself longing for rainy days. I didn't care anymore what anyone else thought. If it was raining and anyone was around me, I mentioned that God loved me. I did get some strange looks—even looks of pity—but I didn't care! The great God of Heaven loved rotten ol' me!

Every time it rains, not only am I reminded of God's love, but I am also reminded that God supplies every need I have. No one else could supply that need we had for water in our city—no scientist, no meteorologist, no water conservationist—only God. When I have a need, I know I can trust God to supply that need. I love the verse in Deuteronomy 2:7 where God tells His people, "...these forty years the LORD thy God hath been with thee; thou hast lacked nothing." That's how I feel—I can't remember a time when God didn't meet every need I have ever had.

I am also reminded that God doesn't let it rain forever. The sun will come out soon. When times of life are hard, I know that God will meet my need. I know that God is with me through the difficult times, and that they won't last too long. God is so good!

I have also learned what a great sense of humor God has. I was scheduled to sing a solo on a Sunday evening in May of 2006. It was Mother's Day, and that Sunday afternoon we actually had a terrible hailstorm and a very severe thunderstorm. It continued to rain into the evening service. Our auditorium has a metal roof, so the sound of rain can be extremely loud. This time it was so loud that the prayer before the song could barely be heard. When I began the song, the sound men had my microphone turned up extra loud to compensate for the noise of the rain. It never dawned on me what song I had chosen until the line of the first verse came out of my mouth. I was singing "I Will Survive" written by Mrs. Barbara Burke, and the first line is "A raging storm has come my way; the rain is pouring down." Well, that was it! The crowd in the auditorium burst into laughter! I could barely keep from laughing myself. I thought, "I will survive all right if I can just get through this song." I guess someone in the auditorium needed that laugh. I did survive, and I knew God loved me!

I do love the rain now, and I am not ashamed to tell others that God shows His love for me when it rains. However, I did ask God for another way in addition to the rain, and He gave me one. Whenever one of my three children gives me a hug without my asking for it, I know God loves me! Two of the best things to me are rain and hugs!

I know those things may seem strange to others, but they mean a whole, whole lot to me because they remind me of God's love! I don't know how God could love me, but I am so glad that He does! Thank you, Mrs. Schaap and Christian Womanhood, for helping God to be more real to me in my life.

– Sharon Finley

43

I have been thinking about this for some time now, and so many things have happened in my life that show how God loves me. First of all, He loved me enough to save my soul.

I am reminded of the time I was driving on the expressway late at night with my two children in the back seat of a very small car. A drunken driver hit us from the rear traveling at least 120 miles per hour. I managed to keep the car on the road and swerve to miss an oncoming car. When the state patrolman saw the damage to our car, he said we should all be dead. My son, who was about ten years old at the time, said, "It was like God put His hand between our car and the drunk driver."

Then I had to think about having breast cancer in my 30s with two young children. My first thought was "Why me? Am I going to die?" When I went in for the biopsy, I was taken to the surgical waiting area where an IV was started. I lay there for quite some time. I became very frightened, and thoughts of death came into my mind. "What if I don't wake up from the anesthesia?" I was almost having a panic attack, seriously thinking about ripping out the IV and running out of there. I started to cry. A nurse came to my side and asked, "Are you okay?"

"NO!" I sobbed.

Then I closed my eyes and began to pray. Within minutes a peace came over me that I had never before felt. It was like Jesus was standing right beside me, holding my hand and telling me everything would be fine. And it was—even though I was diagnosed with malignant breast cancer.

I went back two weeks later for a modified radical mastectomy. This time I had total peace about the whole experience, and God decided to spare my life. That was over 20 years ago.

How does God love me? Let me count the ways!

– Nancy Harwood

44

*W*hen I am having difficulties, sadness, or fears, I close my eyes and climb up on the lap of God—like a little girl would go to her daddy. I can feel the warmth and strength of His arms wrapped around me, and I am once again reminded of the love He has for me as His child and the almighty power He has to help me through whatever I am facing.

– Spring Jeffers

45

*T*o select just one example of God's love for me would be an awesome task. His daily protection, my wonderful family, and the joy He allows us are all showers of blessings. Another sweet way that He really shows His love is through the care of our wonderful Christian friends. One of these whom I have been privileged to love for 20 years is Linda Vaprezsan.

I first met her when we were trying to move to the Belleville area and were looking for housing. She found us a house just a few miles from the church. Even though we were regular church attenders, our children loved riding the bus. We would wait until they were on the bus and then drive to the church. One Sunday, however, the children would get extra points if their parents rode also, so I gritted my teeth and submitted myself to the noise and odors that our dedicated bus workers face every Sunday of the year.

In my then two-year-old son's Sunday school class, they served lunch each week as many of the children come without having had breakfast and have a lengthy bus ride home. That day my son had had breakfast, but he could not believe his good fortune in being allowed to eat all the grapes he could swallow. I picked him up after church, and we got on the bus. Immediately he emptied the contents of his stomach all over himself, me, and a very unfortunate teen worker. Of course, I was mortified as I rushed to a restroom to try to clean up as much as possible.

Suddenly it occurred to me that we were "trapped." I had no car to get home, and I didn't know anyone in the church. I really could not face getting back on the bus. Just as I was planning to walk the distance, in walked Mrs. Vaprezsan. She insisted on driving us home despite the unpleasant mess we were both in. She was so gracious, and I couldn't believe that a pastor's wife would be so quick to help in such an unpleasant situation. (She did get another car soon after, and I always wondered if it was because she could not get the car in which we had ridden properly fumigated!)

She got me back though. A relative of my husband had died, and we really didn't want to have our girls miss school or our son to travel all day. Once again Mrs. Vaprezsan came to the rescue. She offered to watch our son for the day as her son Todd and he were so similar in age. We were really relieved, picking him and the girls up after school, and I was indebted to her again. That is, until around 7:00 that evening when she called to warn us that Todd had just broken out in chicken pox, and Jeff had obviously been exposed.

We still laugh about it because it was the beginning of a dear, dear friendship. Through the years we have shared the joys and tears of watching our children grow up, worked on so many projects together, and even after my husband was transferred, I knew where there was a ready ear.

Mrs. Linda Vaprezsan is a great lady and so terribly busy with all her responsibilities. I am forever humbled that she always seems to have time to be my friend. How could God show more love than that? — Brenda Sharkey

#6

I love yellow VW bugs and sunflowers, and every time I see one of them it reminds me of God's love. I see the "bugs" in all kinds of places—not just on streets. Sometimes they appear in the form of little matchbox-size replicas in stores, or I'll see sunflowers on a greeting card. God is truly good!

— Kimberly Shew

#7

I was driving home on a road that runs along a river with a forested area on the other side of the road. My heart was breaking because a very dear family that had been with us since the starting of our church was moving to another city. We had just been through a very tough time in our church, and I felt that God just kept taking and taking and taking. "*…The LORD gave,* *and the* LORD *hath taken away....* " (Job 1:21) I was overwhelmed with deep sadness, and tears were streaming down my cheeks as I drove. Then as I rounded a curve in the road, there I saw, just as close to the edge of the road as could be, seven or eight deer—just standing there looking at me. It was such a beautiful sight, and God whispered, "I love you, and it will be okay!" as I drove by.   – Cherie Dye

#8

When my mom passed away on October 27, 2005, I didn't think I could get through it. But God not only helped me, He also gave me the strength to help my siblings get through that difficult time. He also shows His love through a great church with such great people. God shows me love through them. I love attending a church where I know that I am loved, and I think that is how God shows His love for me.

– Samantha Montlouis

#9

My first ladies' Spectacular was in 1988. I went with four other ladies in my church. A lady and her husband who were graduates of Hyles-Anderson College had come to our church. I had never heard of the college at that time. She invited me to go with her to the Christian Womanhood Spectacular. I had a four year old and a seven month old at the time. I had thought there was no way I could go. My husband told me that he would love for me to go, and he would take some vacation days from work to keep our daughters.

I reluctantly packed my bags. I had never before left my family overnight, and it was a 13-hour drive each way. It was the greatest decision I have ever made other than my salvation and choosing to marry my husband. The meeting changed my life. I had never heard of Marlene Evans, JoJo Moffitt, Beverly Hyles, or the other ladies who spoke. The theme was "I See Gold Glittering." I bought a lot of books and tapes, and when I got home, I began to put into practice what I had learned.

My husband was so impressed and complimented me so much. I really didn't know what to expect when I went, and I really didn't realize how much I had changed when I came home, but my husband did. When he went to Pastors' School the following March, I wrote him a letter and put it in his suitcase, telling him I would be praying that he would get half as much as I did.

We really didn't know what Pastors' School at First Baptist Church of Hammond, Indiana, was, but he and some men in our church went. On Thursday night of that week, Dr. Jack Hyles preached, "If I Perish, I Perish." My husband was called to preach that night. A year later we headed off to Texas Baptist College.

While I was at the ladies' Spectacular, I bought Mrs. Evans' book *Redbirds and Rubies and Rainbows.* How I love that book. So when Mrs. Schaap told us about what she looked for when God told her that He loved her, I wanted to do that also. I chose redbirds because I love the color red, and I remembered how much my life was changed by Marlene Evans' book and by going to the Spectacular.

Now my husband pastors Grace Baptist Church in Cedar Grove, North Carolina. Our oldest daughter Leslie graduated from Hyles-Anderson College and married Jon Gieseler. Our daughter Emily is now a junior at Hyles-Anderson College and is a member of a summer tour group for the college. Our son Chase is a high school sophomore who plans to attend Hyles-Anderson College and then return to be his dad's assistant.

When I see redbirds, God not only reminds me that He loves me, He is also telling me that He is the greatest thing that has ever happened in my life. God is so good!

– Annette Hamilton

50

Whenever I see bees or yellow VW bug cars, I am reminded that God and my husband love me. Dr. Jack Schaap recently said that he had told God that when he sees a deer, it reminds him that God loves him, but if he had the deer in possession, he would really know God loves him! I liked that, so I told my husband, "You know, Honey, when I see a yellow VW bug, it reminds me that you and God love me, but if I had one in my possession, I would really know you love me!" We got a good laugh out of that comment, but I haven't gotten a car out of it yet—maybe someday!

Pennies are yet another reminder that God loves me. At Christmas I bought sachet bags, glued pennies on them, and enclosed a little note inside that said, "God loves you." I gave one to each teen girl in our youth group and told them to put the pennies they found in the bags. Next year we'll see how many we found.

Hardly a day goes by when I don't find at least one penny or see a yellow bug car. God loves me a whole lot!!

– Heidi Haynes

51

*I*n a third-world country like Nepal, American products are rarely seen anywhere—much less in the local grocery stores. My motto has always been, "It's not American, but it's better than nothing." We've just learned to deal with it. One of the ways God shows His love to me is when my or my families' favorites just happen to appear on the shelves. Such was the case on June 30, 2007. All my hugs from Jesus came all at once. It felt like a bear hug and was even a bit overwhelming.

As we walked down the first aisle, I found my first hug—Dr. Pepper and Diet Dr. Pepper. All I could say was "Wow!" After a few minutes, more hugs came. We found Kraft Miracle Whip, Capri Sun Juices, and Gatorade. Then I glanced up to find one-gallon jars of the biggest dill pickles I have ever seen from the USA. My husband said, "It sure would be nice if God would send us some grape jelly!" Although we were in shock from all that we had already found, we kept walking down the aisles. Sure enough, another hug came along—grape jelly!

Two weeks earlier I had made a carrot cake for my son's

birthday. He really wanted cream cheese icing, but all that was available was vanilla. He was thankful for the vanilla, but I was sorry I couldn't give him what he really wanted. With that said, not far past the grape jelly was our next hug. You guessed it, Betty Crocker cream cheese icing! So I'm off to make another carrot cake.

When God demonstrates His love, He surely does spread His arms wide open! We are not sure how long these things will last on the shelves, but who cares. Nothing can or will change the way God showed His love for me that day.

– Cheri Ortiz

52

I have to say that when I see a cardinal, it really reminds me that God loves me. My mom's favorite bird was the cardinal, so when I see one, I always think of her. It has been eight years since she graduated to Heaven, and I really do miss her. When the Lord allows a cardinal to cross my path, it is like He is saying, "I know you miss your mom, but I am here with you. I love you and care for you."

One day while we were living in Georgia, I was really feeling down, and I looked out at our bird feeders in the backyard and saw at least 18 male cardinals and 10 female cardinals. Wow! My whole outlook changed, and I knew God was watching over me and loved me. – Joyce Kiefer

𝒢od reminds me of His love to me by way of a penny. So many times throughout my life, I have felt very small and unloved. However, God makes me feel loved, and I draw close to Him when I find a penny. May I share some of the places where I've found "God's penny"?

Early in the morning, when I couldn't sleep and decided to put a load of laundry in the washer, a penny lay in the empty washing machine. How excited I was! Just before I got into my van to run an errand, I found a penny lying on my seat. I have found them on the floor in the check-out lane of the grocery store, on the ground in the church parking lot, in my driveway, in my husband's trousers' pockets, and the list could go on and on. Some ladies are reminded of God's love through rainbows or hummingbirds, but God gives me pennies many times throughout the week just to remind me that He cares and He's always there. How precious we are to Him! Matthew 10:31 says, *"Fear ye not therefore, ye are of more value than many sparrows."* – Valerie Frey

54

ℐt is very difficult to choose just one particular story of how God shows His love to me in a small way, and I'm stumped because He does big things all the time in my life!

The year 2002 was a devastating year of deaths in the family with the loss of my husband's only uncle, my sister-in-law, and my nephew. My mother-in-law was stricken with MS, and another nephew was in a coma from a horrific car accident. My children were devastated, and I've never seen them cry so much from one tremendous blow after another. With each incident we prayed, and we leaned on God and each other. With all that had already happened, my husband was involved in a car crash with a fatality on December 31, 2002. The driver of the offending car was killed. I hoped that the driver at least had trusted Christ as Saviour before that day.

To make a long story short, three months into my husband's recovery, we were broke. We had no money left in the bank and no food in the fridge. It was a Friday night, and I was praying silently to myself while watching the kids and making sure they were quiet so my husband could rest. The doorbell rang. It was my son's Boy Scout den leader and his wife, and they brought in two huge boxes of franks and beans left over from the jamboree they had had that night. I was so happy I cried. We had enough food to last two weeks, and my kids had the biggest smiles on their faces. See, I told you GOD does BIG things for me all the time.   – Johanna Bright

55

I have always loved hummingbirds, and I know Mrs. Cindy Schaap is reminded of God's love when she sees them. But I never thought God would use them to show me He loves me.

This past year has been one of the most difficult years we

have experienced. Our brother-in-law was diagnosed with inoperable brain cancer; our little grandson Evan was born with a very rare skin disease, and we nearly lost him four times. I had back surgery; my mom, who has a kidney disease and heart disease, was diagnosed with cancer (I am her caregiver); our home flooded three times; plus countless other things. There have been times when I have honestly felt overwhelmed.

About a week ago my husband and I were having devotions together on our back deck. A hummingbird flew a foot or so in front of him and hovered there looking at him. He flew to where I was sitting and did the same to me. He then flew to the feeder and began to drink. A few days ago I was walking through my living room and heard a buzzing sound by the window. There was our hummingbird friend trapped inside our house. I walked to the window and reached out for him. I held him in my hands. He sat very still and didn't try to fly away.

I walked him over to the door and let him go. I felt in my heart the Lord telling me "Eileen, you don't care for that bird any more than I care for you. Just trust Me and rest in My hands. I know the beginning from the end. It's in MY control." Praise the Lord, we can learn that God loves us from even the smallest of His creatures. 　　　　　　　 – Eileen Abberger

56

When I open my eyes early in the morning, I see sunlight streaming through the window—a daily reminder that my God is an amazing Creator. He allows me to witness the beauty of

His creation each morning and drink in the warmth of His light—a demonstration of His great love. Then, I look at my wonderful husband, and I am continually reminded how God precisely and lovingly brought my husband and me together through circumstances that He alone could master. He not only gave me a special husband, but He gave me a husband who is a fantastic preacher and a kind, compassionate pastor. God has used my husband to teach me, challenge me, and encourage me in my walk with the Lord—another daily reminder of how God loves me.

Ephesians 3:20a says, *"Now unto him that is able to do exceeding abundantly above all that we ask or think...."* God has certainly shown me in ways I never could have imagined that He loves me. The love of God is greater far than tongue can tell, so my words are definitely inadequate when it comes to expressing how God loves me. He is SO good!

– Donna Stewart

57

I don't really like to borrow special things from others; I want them to be my own. However, a strange thing happened to me that made me think of the Lord's watch care over me. I dropped my purse in my front yard one night, and sure enough, in the morning all my cash and most of my change was gone—all but the pennies!

Even though I was upset and angry at myself for doing such a thing, it reminded me of Pastor Jack Schaap and his penny story. It always brings a slight smile to me when I think that the thief left me all the pennies—what a blessing!

– Lisa Downing

58

*T*his may seen like a very silly way to remember that God loves me, but to a "shopaholic" like myself, it is a very real and wonderful way. Shopping is my way of relaxing, although some need to relax after shopping. So for me, a day at the mall or in multiple stores is great fun—even if I am only "shop looking." Sometimes the way I remember God loves me and is always looking out for me is the times when I find the deals of a lifetime. I will have to take you back to December of last year.

While Christmas shopping at a local up-scale shopping center (I don't buy much there, but it is always fun to look!), I entered the Anne Taylor shop. They always have so many nice things that I try to get some ideas from them. While there, I spotted a gorgeous $80 skirt, and to say the least, it was way out of my price range. So I just drooled a bit and eventually left the shop.

After Christmas, thinking we might find some good deals, my family and I went back to the same shopping center. Again we entered the Anne Taylor shop. I looked everywhere for the "skirt of my dreams," hoping it had gone on sale. (My dad was buying this time!) But alas, it was nowhere to be found, and the workers did not even remember this dream skirt. Oh, well. On to another shop! Don't worry because this whole time God was thinking of me and loving me more than I could ever imagine!

Just two days ago my mom, my sister, my niece and I went to a Salvation Army store in our area. We had been told that it was a really nice one, and it was. It was so organized and had really nice items—not just the typical "nobody-else-wants-it-either" junk. We all found many good deals. But I took the cake, or as the cashier put it, "This is a time I like to say, 'You go girl!'" God had a present waiting there just for me. I found my $80 dream skirt, in my size, hanging in the Salvation Army store! It was brand-new with the original $80 store tags still on it, and I paid only $8 for it!

I am so amazed at how God did all that for me. As I have said before, some may not think that this is a legitimate or a good way to remember that God loves me, but finding amazing deals like this (and not always while shopping) always reminds me that God loves me, He is always there with me, and He is always looking out for my best interest.

– Bethany Cox

59

My husband drove a public school bus for seven years to help get our church off the ground. The first year that he took a full-time salary from the church was a rough financial year for us. Our three children were small, and they were not spoiled with having things. However, on their birthdays and Christmas, we had become accustomed to doing some nice things for them.

The first Christmas my husband worked for the church full-time, I was very concerned about the kind of Christmas we would have. Our daughter Catharine had asked for a desk, and our son Joey had asked for a car he could pedal and drive. Christmas was just two weeks away, and we still did not have our car and desk or the funds available to buy them. I was getting very concerned.

On Saturday our eight-month-old daughter Amanda and I were visiting for my Sunday school class. As I was driving down a street, I prayed and said, "Dear God, you know how much I love You. I've given my life to serve You. Please give me a car and a desk for our children."

I turned right after the stop sign, and there they were! A brand new Playskool desk and a shiny black Kett-Kar were sitting at the end of someone's driveway with a sign on them that said, "FREE"! I loaded them in my minivan as quickly as I could, thanking God and crying the whole time. I am still amazed when I think about the looks I saw on our children's faces that Christmas morning when they received those gifts.

– Amy Vassak

60

It may seem strange to some that I really don't have a specific thing for which I look that reminds me that God loves me. Each day is a new day God has given me, and each day something will happen that tells me He loves me. For instance, I do all the planning for our Mother-Daughter banquets. I am not a great idea person, but God knows that, so I just tell Him I need an idea. Before too long, He will give me an idea that is just great! It usually comes in just a phrase I hear or something I see that all of the sudden says, "Here is what you need to do!" Two years ago my husband and I got so excited because I knew that our banquet should be "The Apple of His Eye," and the speaker should be Mrs. Janice Morgan from the "Big Apple"—New York. We served a New York deli menu.

The banquet was great. After it was over, I was trying to think of next year's theme when I pulled into our garage and saw the sign that said "There's No Place Like Home." That is our theme for next year, and our speaker will be Mrs. Debi Young from Hammond, which is my home. Also, she represents our home missions—Hyles-Anderson College. The menu will be a down-home cookout.

I could go on and on, but this is the way it goes. Two years ago we did "Follow the Son," and our speaker was Mrs. Kelly Johnson from Japan, the land of the rising sun. Our decorations were all sunflowers, and our food was oriental.

These past few weeks while I have been laid up with foot surgery, God has showed me many times that He loves me. Our ladies have been so kind to me with bringing meals, cleaning my house, doing the ironing, etc.

One evening when I was home alone, the doorbell rang. Dave Prater and Paul Johnson had brought me a beautiful petunia hanging plant. I was overwhelmed with their thoughtfulness. These two widowed men had thought of me, and I knew God loved me.

Then a few days later when feeling very weary, I received a surprise delivery of a beautiful fruit arrangement from the ladies of Christian Womanhood. God surely loves me.

As you can see, God shows me He loves me in many different ways—on a daily basis.   – Linda Vaprezsan

61

*G*od has shown His love to me in numerous ways. I believe the most unique and amazing way was when He saved me. I was an addict and an alcoholic, addicted to crack cocaine and living in the streets. I had no hope and nowhere to turn (or so I thought). Years of sexual, mental, and physical abuse left me with little security about myself. I had guns pulled on me and had witnessed everything from gang rape to murder. I gave birth to three children out of wedlock. My family would have nothing to do with my children much less me, because of their mixed race. How could I expect a God in Heaven to even consider a drug-addicted prostitute like myself?

I was at the end of my rope, trying to drown myself in drugs and sin. My children were lost to the government, even though temporarily in my family's care. I ended up in jail for the more than the twentieth time in 28 years. When some ladies wearing long skirts came on a Thursday night from some church, I thought they were Pentecostal. As I watched them, I observed God's love though them.

It took maybe a month, through many questions and discussions, but in September 2000 I accepted God's greatest gift of love—His Son Jesus. Since that time, God has shown me His love in ways I never thought possible. I am under the preaching of the best pastor, Brother Jimmy McCullough. (He ranks right up there with Dr. Jack Schaap!)

I now own my own home and live there with my three children. I work on the church bus route and in children's church. I teach fourth through sixth grade girls in Sunday school, and I serve as the secretary and assistant counsel leader for Reformers Unanimous, an addiction program sponsored by our church. I am even trusted with secretarial duties for our church.

When I was first saved through the outreach of Bethel Baptist Church in Walls, Mississippi, I attended Tri-State Baptist College nearly two years. I have been under the ministry of Pastor Jimmy McCullough in Coldwater, Mississippi, for nearly five years. God is love, and He has shown me how I can accept His love and give it to others in return. The road is sometimes lonely and not always easy, but I always have hope and God's love to lean on. – Cynthia Bailey

62

I am a member of the adult choir at First Baptist Church of Hammond, Indiana. One day while I was in choir practice before church on a Wednesday evening, someone asked me how I was doing, and I just happened to mention that I wasn't feeling very well. The next Sunday this wonderful lady asked me how I was feeling, and then she added that she was praying for me. I felt Jesus wrapping His arms around me with a great big hug and saying "I love you." At the time, I didn't know this lady's name or she my name, but to this day I pray for her and she prays for me. I felt really loved and special that day to Jesus.

My friend of 25 years, Rema Vezey, is the most generous person I know. One Sunday when she arrived in the Friendship Sunday School Class, I complimented her beautiful necklace. The next Sunday she gave me a necklace just like it but a different color. I was so thrilled with the gift and how our Heavenly Father uses others to show His love for me. Once again I felt His arms around me telling me He loves me. What a great Father I have.   – Becky Wolfe

63

The day I saw one of those bracelets to which you connect charms. I just thought in my mind, "I would like one of those." Almost immediately after that thought, I walked around the corner and a friend of mine, whom I only see once a year, handed me a small bag, and she said, "This is for you from me." Inside was one of those charm bracelets, and she had put two charms on it.

I didn't even tell anyone I wanted one! I just had a thought! I knew God was saying, "I love you, Patty! You're special to Me!" It was not a need; it was just a thought—a want. And immediately God gave me a treat. He loves to give surprises to His children, just like we do sometimes. I was so excited. I knew God was letting me know, "I'm thinking of you today! I love you!"

I know that God loves me when I realize that I have His Word! I have been led in paths of righteousness all of my life because His Word was passed down to relatives and then to me.

It has proven true every time, and the words of comfort, strength, and tenderness assure me of God's love every day of my life. Why would I not want to read it? It contains the words of love that I crave! His Love Letter, my Bible, is the sweet expressions of the eternal love of God! YES! Jesus loves me! The Bible tells me so!

One day my heart was broken in a million pieces. When that happened, I got up and went to my usual place of prayer. At that time, it was kneeling by the couch in the very early hours of the morning. I was so hurt that I did not even have words to say. I just knelt and quietly wept. The weight of pain on my heart and mind was more than I could bear. As I knelt with my head on the couch, it was as if the Lord Jesus Himself came. My head was on His lap, and He was caressing my hair. He did not speak either, but He came to me. No, I was not losing my mind. God came to me in my time of need. He made His presence known by His Spirit. I was comforted.

He loved me tenderly that morning. I was able to stop crying, and my burden became His. I'll never forget that morning when He was so real and I was given the love of an eternal God and compassionate Saviour. His Word and love are true (John 14: 16-18). Of course, I know God loves me!

It is so fun to look back over the day and see the work that you've accomplished and realize that it was God Who helped you do it. It is at that moment that I know God's strength and grace and I can say, "Thank You, God. It's been a good day! I am glad that you love me enough to help me in the work that You have given me!"

It is impossible to think that God doesn't love me when I

consider that He gives me my physical life—without any help from me. I know that God loves me when I consider that He keeps my heart beating and my lungs breathing all the night long while I sleep and throughout the day—without any conscious effort on my part. My very existence is dependent on Him! I understand from Colossians 1 that all things consist by Him and were created for Him! What love!! Of course, I KNOW that He loves ME! I am His beloved creation, and my physical body is proof!

I know that God loves me because He lets me serve Him. To understand that a sinner can be useful in the kingdom of Heaven is truly the love of God. Jesus has given us the responsibility of the greatest treasure on earth—the Gospel. It is not a light thing that He lets us have a part! It is ultimate joy as a Christian to get to serve Him knowing what a sinner I am! What love! I know God loves me when I get to teach my beginners about Him, or set up chairs for a Sunday school class, or wipe off a table so that others may come and find out that God loves them too! Only God so lovingly gives us that opportunity and lets us be a part of His very body. His Word says that I am HIS hands. I am HIS eyes. I am HIS ears. That He would let me be a representative of Himself is the ultimate expression of love, grace, and mercy! I know God loves me!!

I know that God loves me when I consider the fact that He placed me in the great country of America. The heritage of this land is a gift that was bought with much sacrifice, love, dedication, and prayer. The United States of America was founded by Him, and I get to enjoy it every day. What love!!!

I know that God loves me when my eyes can behold my

husband. To see my husband's face and to let our eyes meet is the kindness and love of God. Yes, I know God loves me, even if I did not have a husband, but each day that I get to share in my husband's life shows the care and love of God extended to me. And I have eyes that can behold the one I love the most on earth. I know that it is the love of God to me. Each day with my husband is God's saying, "I love you Patty. You mean so much to me that I will let you share in Kevin's life." Kevin's love is the real, tangible evidence of God's love for me.

I know that God loves me when I consider that I am the temple not only of God, but that my body was made to be a temple for a little baby. God made woman to be the home of a baby for nine months. If God has let you have this experience of bearing a child, you realize the tender love of God as you feel the baby, see and feel your belly move, and realize that your body is the temple of a life. A child is the fruit of love, and nothing shows God's love more than a baby. I know God loves me because He has let me be the temple and care for three children, and I get to nourish and train them. What LOVE!!!

I am not always the best when it comes to making purchases. Sometimes I can be impulsive when I think something is a good buy. In other words, I don't always think it through. Thankfully, my husband is just the opposite. For my birthday, I was given some money. I was so excited. I knew exactly what I wanted. I had been wanting a painting of a covered bridge for my living room. I set aside a day when I would go shopping for the picture. I had my eye on another print for the same amount of money that I had been given. As I looked at it, I wasn't sure if I wanted to spend all of my money on it because it was not a picture of a covered bridge, so I thought I would be good and wait. I looked around our area stores, but I couldn't find what I wanted. Then I remembered a local artist who is a Christian lady. I went to her house, told her the amount of money I had and what I wanted. She said she could not do it for that price, so I declined. After returning home, I was sort of disappointed that I had not found what I wanted. When I got home, there was a message on our answering machine from that same local artist. She said that she would do it for my price. I was so excited that I went back, and we decided what would be best. It seemed like everything was perfect!

I waited about a month for her to complete the painting, and then I went to pick it up. She met me at a picture frame shop, and now we needed to pick out a frame for it. The painting was good—not exactly what I had in mind, but I still liked it. Then she proceeded to give me the costs of frames and mats for it. It was a lot more than the painting, and she put much pressure on me to get what she suggested. Because I do not like to hurt people's feelings, I finally conceded to her wishes. BIG MISTAKE! When I went to pick up the picture, framed and matted, it was three times the amount she had estimated in the beginning! I had to pay it, and I was very upset. Because I do not work outside the home, I knew my husband would not be pleased with me, and now he was going to be stuck with a bill for something that was really not important and definitely not a need. I felt so bad.

When I got home, I went for a walk. I sat down on the grass and talked to the Lord. I said in my heart, "Lord, I've done it again. Why can't I be trusted to make good purchases! I wish I could just do better! Jesus, please forgive me for putting this burden on my husband. And please, work this out somehow."

The next week I was able to do some things for a friend. When I was done, that friend, to my surprise, gave me the exact amount that I needed to pay for my picture! (My friend knew nothing about it!) When I opened my envelope and saw what the amount was for my services, I was reminded that God loved me!! He took care of my foolishness again! He forgave me, as He so mercifully does again and again. Of course God loves me. He forgiveth all my iniquities (Psalm 103:3) and shows me such compassion and forgiveness. Yes, God loves me! *"Like as a father pitieth his children, so the LORD pitieth them that fear him."* (Psalm 103:13) I am glad I have God to help me—even when I mess up! What a Saviour Who loves even ME!!!

– Patty Albert

64

Seeing digits on the clock that are exactly the same is my reminder that God loves me. I can be buzzing around the house multitasking with a million things on my mind, glance quickly at the clock, and notice it reads "2:22" or "10:10." To me, a bonus is when I catch it at "11:11"! Sometimes there is no way to describe it but amazing!

For instance, the last time we were attending a conference at Metro Baptist Church in Belleville, Michigan, we were eating at Cracker Barrel. I heard a cell phone ring, and thinking it was mine, I naturally reached in my purse only to find that it wasn't. However, the time on my phone read "5:55."

There are times when I might have a particularly heavy heart, glance at my cell phone to see what time it is, and see it is "3:33." About a year and a half ago, we had a young lady from our church attending Hyles-Anderson College. She was dating a young man whom we had met, and they were practicing all the proper dating standards. One day I asked God something like this, "God, You know how we feel about Vicky. You know we love her and want only the very best for her. You know how people present themselves in the best light possible, and naturally people try to make good impressions. God, I don't know him personally. God, if there is any reason why Vicky should not be dating this young man, could You somehow reveal this to me?"

I prayed this prayer during the holiday season, and within a very short amount of time, Vicky's boyfriend called. For some reason I did not hear my cell phone ring, so when my phone alerted me that I had a message, I listened as I normally do. The message from Alberto thanked my husband and me for leading Vicky to the Lord. He also expressed his gratitude for the influence we had had in her life. It did my heart good that he would take time out of his schedule to just call to thank us. Oh yes, and the time of the call was "4:44" p.m.! I took that as a clear sign from God that Alberto was the right person for Vicky, and they are now happily married and will eventually be serving in Ecuador as missionaries.

One more thing! My sign that God loves me is not limited to just exact digits on the clock. It could be any exact digits. All my life I prayed for twins. My husband and I were not even able to conceive. We celebrated our tenth-year wedding anniversary the summer our first son Michael was born. I remember realizing how much work one child was and said "Thank You" to God for saying "No" to twins the first time. Just a few years later I ended up having twins—identical twins—after all!

– Donna Murray

65

𝒯he summer of 1994 found our family living in Easley, South Carolina. We were between churches (I hate that term), and we had moved to the South from the U.P. of northern Michigan. We moved to the South with broken hearts. It was not a happy time. My preacher husband had to return to the tool and die trade in which he had worked since high school. God had used this trade to support our family during the college years at Hyles-Anderson College. And now after 14 years of not being a tool and die maker, my husband would return to that trade. Each day as my husband would leave for work, he would cry, and I would say, "Honey, you are a master tool and die maker and look how God is using you in the lives of the men in the shop."

He would say, "God didn't call me to be a tool and die maker; He called me to pastor." Then he would leave for work.

I would also add that immediately upon our arrival, the pastor of the church that we joined handed over his adult Sunday school class to my husband. Technically, in my mind, he was still preaching. The people in the church loved us. (I no longer felt like we had a "bull's eye" on our backs.)

I was going to start teaching kindergarten in the Christian school, and the last two of our six children, the only ones still at home, were excited about starting a new school. "My children and I are happy," I thought. "Couldn't my husband be happy too?"

When we left Michigan, I insisted upon bringing a beautiful fuchsia plant that I had purchased from our Christian school plant sale. We took turns holding it on the way, and it survived to see the South. I hung the plant on the wide front porch of the house that God had miraculously given us to rent, and it thrived. I was sitting on the porch swing early one morning praying and thinking about all that had so suddenly come into our lives when a movement around the plant caught my eye. It was a hummingbird! I had never seen a hummingbird in real life. But I saw one now! That bird and his friends came back all summer and into the fall. They stayed as long as the fuchsia bloomed, and that was until Thanksgiving! The next spring I purchased a new fuchsia plant, and the birds came back.

In September of 1995 my husband received a call from an evangelist friend who told him of a church in Michigan needing a pastor. The evangelist wanted to recommend my husband. I DID NOT want him to recommend my husband. We had settled into a routine. I did not want to go back. But I trusted my husband then as I had always trusted him, and we did make the trip north for him to meet the people and candidate. We immediately fell in love with the people, and they with us. He was called and by late September of 1995, we were again back in the ministry.

In January of 1996 my mother suffered a sudden heart

attack, and three days later went to be with the Lord. She had been a blessing and encouragement all of my life. She kept us well supplied with canned vegetables and other goodies all through our college days. She and my dad loved Dr. Jack Hyles and First Baptist Church of Hammond, Indiana. In fact, they were both sweetly saved and baptized on an Easter Sunday shortly after we had joined the staff at First Baptist Church of Hammond, Indiana, in 1980. They loved the Best Year's Club (for adults age 50 and older) and would travel from their home in Michigan to be a part of the activities. When my husband left First Baptist Church to go into the pastorate in 1985, they continued to encourage us and be a part of the churches that my husband pastored. I was heartbroken and dearly missed my mother.

In the spring of the same year we found that my dad had colon cancer. I was the first girl after two boys, and I can honestly say that Dad loved me best! He was my friend and buddy. I was devastated at the news. I was sitting in our family room one day and again, just as in the South, a movement outside the patio doors caught my eye. It was a hummingbird! Only this time there was no fuchsia plant to attract a hummingbird. My South Carolina bird friends had followed me to Michigan!

I immediately ran to the store for a hummingbird feeder and called someone in our church to find out the ratio of sugar and water. I believe with all of my heart that just as in South Carolina, God was letting me know that though I had suffered deep grief and would suffer more grief in the near future, He would always be there. My dad was able to visit on several occasions and enjoy my hummingbirds with me. Those times together remain precious memories that I cherish. Dad passed away in August—just eight months after Mom. I was now an "orphan."

My hummingbirds have come back each spring for the last 12 years. If I am discouraged, I can look out my kitchen window, and one or more will be at the feeder. If I'm feeling negative, they remind me to be positive. As they squabble with each other, they make me laugh.

When we were at First Baptist Church of Hammond, Indiana, I loved to hear Brother Ray Boardway sing, "There Is a Balm in Gilead," and the choir would join in at the chorus. My hummingbirds are like a balm to my soul. I loved it when Mrs. Schaap sang, "He Loves Me Like I Was His Only Child" at a Christian Womanhood Spectacular a couple of years ago; the hummingbirds remind me of that love.

Do I still have trials, grief, discouragement, and disappointments in my life? Absolutely! Don't we all? Do I wish to be back in South Carolina with a tool and die maker husband and my teaching kindergarten? Not for a moment! I'm thankful for the journey and that God has loved me enough to patiently teach me and always remind me that He truly does "love me like I was His only child."   – Roberta Wertz

66

I know God loves me when we receive a letter or phone call from one of our five children. Just the sound of their voices blesses our hearts. We miss them but are thankful they are all serving the Lord where He has placed them. Their touching base with us shows they care enough to let us in on their lives and what they are doing. God's love connects us.

– Helen MacCormack

67

On Sunday, April 12, 1996, we were starting our Sunday school in the church my husband had founded. Our oldest daughter was just a baby, and although the church was doing fairly well financially for its size, our personal finances were not. It had taken every penny we had to move to New York from Indiana, get settled, and get our church off the ground. My husband was driving a school bus to help support our family and working a couple of side jobs as well.

To kick off our Sunday school, my husband had invited some special guests to be with us for services on Friday night, Saturday, and Sunday. We were worn out from all of the planning, visiting, and all the details that go into special meetings. It didn't help that we were new at it.

We came home on Friday night very late and very exhausted. We opened the door to our basement apartment and quickly discovered that our power had been shut off. We wanted to sit down and cry, but my husband quickly went to work stringing an extension cord from an outlet in the laundry area into our apartment so we could at least have some light. My husband was so aggravated, and while we were trying to be positive, we were not being very successful.

We went up the stairs to get the mail. We really didn't want to, but it was something to do. My husband pulled out an envelope from the stack of mail, and his face turned really white. He showed me the envelope with 523 Sibley Street, Hammond, Indiana, in the upper left corner. We knew something special was in that envelope. My husband opened it to find a handwritten letter from Dr. Jack Hyles.

Dear Joe,
I hope you have a great day on April 12. You are a great guy and very special to me. I miss seeing you and Amy around here. I am so proud of you, and by the way, I saw you at Pastors' School and am glad you were here.
Jack Hyles
Daniel 12:3

This would not be the last time that God used Brother Hyles to show us just how much He loves us.

– Amy Vassak

68

My husband and I were married on August 19, 2006. I already had a 13-year-old daughter, so my daughter and I moved from our home and church in Sacramento to Ventura, California, where my husband is the youth pastor of Fundamental Baptist Church. The move was hard for us because we loved our home church. However, we knew that it was God's will, and He had provided us with a man of God to lead our home, as well as having a great church in Ventura.

Because my husband and I were both 35 years of age, we did not want to wait too long to have a baby. We both prayed for God to give us a little one when it was His will to do so. In April we found out that we would be having a baby in December. We couldn't believe it; it all seemed so unreal. Why would He give me such a blessing as this?

Not long after I discovered I was expecting, I became very ill from an ulcerative colitis relapse. I became dehydrated several times and lost ten pounds. I was hospitalized for ten days in May. I really do not like hospitals, I do not like having my blood taken, and I don't like being sick. I am a big baby and a big whiner when I am sick. I was not happy with the whole experience, but God worked it out for good—just like He promises.

During this time, I watched my daughter and my husband's relationship change. They were forced to spend ten days together without Mom. I watched them grow closer together, and what a blessing when my daughter referred to him as her father. I also saw my church family rally around my family, and through this time of illness, both my daughter and I became closer to them and began to feel like a part of them.

After I left the hospital, I was still very weak and unable to do much. My husband and daughter took such great care of me. After being home for a month, my colitis was going into remission. I began to gain weight. However, in mid-June things changed again. When I went to the doctor, the ultrasound showed that I had placenta previa. The doctor ordered limited activity, with the hopes that over the next couple of months the placenta would move to its proper place.

Even with limited activity, I began to bleed heavily. I went to the hospital and returned home with orders for complete bed rest. I was trying very hard not to be discouraged. I was trying to use flip-side thinking—looking for the positive—but it was hard.

I did find something for which to praise God—another ultrasound revealed that the baby was doing fine with a strong heartbeat. However, the placenta had completely attached to the uterine wall and would not move. With this discovery, the doctor ordered bed rest for the next six months of my pregnancy. I was only allowed to walk to the bathroom and shower once a day. Someone had to stay with me 24 hours a day.

God proved Himself faithful, and my husband's job allowed him to work from home. The ladies in the church offered to take turns sitting with me so my husband and daughter could attend church. They also took turns preparing meals for us. I do have to admit that I was feeling somewhat sorry for myself though. During my six months of bed rest, I would miss my daughter's fourteenth birthday, teen camp, a family vacation to visit my parents, the Thanksgiving holidays, and Christmas shopping. However, I knew that the gift of life we would receive in December would be well worth any sacrifice. In using this thought as my encouragement, things began to look up.

After two weeks on complete bed rest, I woke from a nap on June 30 to find that I was bleeding heavily and having contractions. As we drove to the hospital, I felt that our baby had gone to Heaven, but our doctor told us that everything should be fine. "This is just something to do with the placenta previa," he assured us.

I was somewhat confused because I felt God had been preparing my heart for the worst on the way there. Later our doctor couldn't find a heartbeat, so he ordered another ultrasound. We discovered that our sweet little one had indeed gone to Heaven. You feel so helpless and hopeless as you watch the ultrasound screen and see no movement. God's grace was sufficient for us just as He promised.

I had to remain in the hospital for surgery because I was 15 weeks along in my pregnancy. The first night the doctor prescribed a medicine to cause contractions and Demerol to relieve the pain. Every four hours the nurses gave me a shot of Demerol, and as I started to go to sleep, I began thinking of Obed-edom in II Samuel. Why? I don't know because I had not heard a sermon about him, nor had I recently read about him. I only know that thinking of Obed-edom gave me such a peace through that first night and comforted my heart.

The next day before surgery I said to my husband, "I have no idea why, but I kept thinking about Obed-edom and the ark. I have thought about him all night and all day." During my surgery, my husband looked it up in the Bible. When I got back to my room, my husband then shared the whole story of Obed-edom with me. You see, David brought the ark to Obed-edom's house, and God left it in his care for three months. While it was in his house, the Bible says that God blessed him. Even when God removed the ark from his house, II Samuel 6:11 and 12 says He continued to bless him and all that pertained to him. I Chronicles 15:24 says Obed-edom was a doorkeeper in the house of God, and I Chronicles 26:8 says that his sons and sons' sons were able men of strength for the Lord's service.

My husband's sharing the story of Obed-edom spoke to my heart in a way I had never before experienced. I had been three months pregnant, and for some reason, God had entrusted me with a little life—even if it was just for a short time. His choice to take our baby seemed to say to me that He was promising to care for my family, He would continue to bless us, and He would bless our future generations. I couldn't believe it at first. I got chills and began to cry—tears of grace and peace. It was as if God had reached His arms down from Heaven and wrapped them around me. I have never felt God's love more than at this time in my life.

When I couldn't think to pray because of medication, He gave me what I needed to make it through. He remained so faithful to me and kept His promises even though I didn't deserve it. He loved me and held me so close. He kept me under the shadow of His wings. He showed me that His grace far surpasses my understanding.

My life since then has changed so much. I now have a closer walk with the Lord—closer than I have had in years. I now have a desire to talk with Him every day and to read His Word. I have also seen a change in my husband and daughter's relationship with the Lord. We still don't understand why God chose to take our baby Home, but we have a peace that this is His will and this is what He felt best. We still know that God loves us beyond our wildest imagination and that He will keep His promises to us. *"Know therefore that the LORD thy God, he is God, the faithful God, which keepeth covenant and mercy with them that love him and keep his commandments to a thousand generations."* (Deuteronomy 7:9)   – Sharon Martin

69

*A*bout ten years ago my daughter, whose husband is a youth pastor, challenged me to write a fictional book for teenage girls that would inspire them to live separated lives. Always during the years since I started it, the question that frequently entered my mind was who would publish it without changing it by watering down the standards of the fundamental, independent Baptist movement? When I finally sent it to Christian Womanhood, I knew I didn't have to worry about that, but I was afraid to hope that they would publish it!

On January 30, 2007, Linda Stubblefield called me with the news that Christian Womanhood would be publishing my book, *A Time to Choose.* My family and many of my friends had been praying with me about getting it published—even before sending it to Christian Womanhood—and now God had answered. This was one of the greatest days of my life. I wrote in my journal: "I am astonished…and I praise the great and mighty God and my 'Abba, Father.' " I love Him so much, and He actually loves little ol' sinful me!   – Yvonne Coats

70

*D*aily as I read the Bible, God's promises are easy to believe. However, sometimes when a trial hits like a sudden storm, my belief then must turn to trust. During one particular trial which came my way, my trust was weak. I claimed Job 6:8, which says,

"Oh that I might have my request; and that God would grant me the thing that I long for!" I prayed day after day for one and one-half years with wavering faith. I could not see how good could come from this trial. I then added this to my prayers, "God, help thou mine unbelief."

God's love for me was evident in the peace and the calm in my heart. I now trusted Him with a strength that only He could give. My nights were still sleepless, yet the relationship between my Lord and me grew deeper. I am thankful that I chose to trust Him instead of blaming Him.

Oh, by the way, the thing for which I longed was that my youngest son would come home. Praise the Lord! He came with a repentant heart. You may ask what the good out of this was. He stayed faithful in doing right, and God brought a friend back into his life whom he had known as a freshman in college. My son James married this Christian girl named Charity Roberts, and after another year, he moved back to Hyles-Anderson College to finish what he had started seven years earlier.

The greatest "good" is the assurance that I am never alone. God is always near. How do I know He loves me? He has promised that He would; I can believe and trust His Word—not because good came from this but because He loves me and knows what is best.   – Cynthia Bell

71

*I*t was Christmas 1992. It had been a very difficult, heart-wrenching year. My husband and I were actively serving the

Lord in the ministry. I was teaching junior high full-time; he was teaching at the college. We had a strong, flourishing ministry. Hundreds, yea thousands of people's lives were being affected yearly. God's hand of blessing was evident on my husband's life and ministry.

Then things began to change. He was no longer satisfied with me, his ministry, or his life. Little by little, he began to change until that fateful day that I came home and found a note on the table, telling me our marriage was over and that he was leaving. He loved someone else.

I was devastated; everything I loved in the world was gone. In the weeks and months that followed, I watched as our ministry and the people in whom we had invested faltered—never to be recovered for the cause of Christ. Besides my personal anguish and pain, I also carried the guilt of the lives which had been ruined because of our failure. I personally visited the home of each of the people over whom we had had influence to tell them of my husband's decision. Our new home was sold, and I was moved into a small apartment near the school.

I was in deep agony and pain. For months I had cried out to God for strength for each day. It was now Christmas Eve 1992. I was all alone in my small apartment, and I was pouring out my lonely heart to God. I was so alone and so brokenhearted. I was crying profusely and asking God if He loved me. "Do You see me? Do You care about me?" I heard a knock on my door.

"Who would be knocking on my door on Christmas Eve?" I wiped my face and tried to appear normal as I opened the door. Standing at the door was a lady from our church. She said that she and her husband wanted to come by and bring me a

Christmas card. I thanked her and closed the door. I laid the card on the table and continued my anguished cry to the Lord.

When I could cry no more, I got up to prepare for bed. I remembered the card and wandered into the kitchen to open it. Inside that card were five $100 bills. I had never even seen a $100 bill, and now I had five of them! Wow! My heart sang for joy! God did love me! He did care! He did see me!

"Does Jesus care when I've said 'goodbye'
To the dearest on earth to me,
And my sad heart aches
Till it nearly breaks,
Is it aught to Him? Does He See?
O yes, He cares, I know He cares,
His heart is touched with my grief...."

– Belinda Gaona

72

Years ago when Grandma Lindner passed into Heaven, my mother laid out before me Grandma's little jewelry trinkets. She offered me my choice of whatever I wanted. Immediately I chose a bright, multi-colored rhinestone butterfly pin. My choice surprised my mother who thought I'd rather have something my grandmother had worn a lot. I guess this pin was something Grandma had found at one of the last garage sales she visited and had never worn.

But that inexpensive, common piece of jewelry held special value to me in that moment of reflection on her life. It was as if she had unknowingly bought that pin for me, her granddaughter, to wear and to remember her thereby. Now I feel God's love when I wear that pin. People always admire the brightly colored butterfly. It is then that I smile, and with thoughts of love, I say, "It's from my grandma who is now in Heaven. She was always a bright spot in my life."

"Pennies in the chicken" is another reason why Grandma was such a bright spot in my life. Every child needs a grandmother like mine who lived in a farmhouse in the country. Mom, Dad, and all four of us kids would load into the car for a ride to Grandma and Grandpa's house. We would run into the kitchen to see what Grandma had for us, and she would say, "Have you been good? Then look and see if you can find my chicken. Maybe she has a gift for you."

My older sister Gina, who was ten years old, would usually be the first to find the hen. A milk glass chicken dish sat in the cupboard, and when Gina lifted the lid, the four of us saw one bright new penny—just one for her. She was thrilled, but my heart fell. There were four of us—didn't the chicken know? And at six years of age, I was just sure that I was the best behaved of all.

Grandma noticed and said, "You can each look a little later on, and maybe my hen will have one for you too."

Her words made sense to me for I reasoned that laying pennies must be harder than laying eggs. Still, I feared I would be left out. So I just kept checking the hen, and sure enough Grandma's hen gave me one too!

Then after the "magical" fun, we sat down to visit in the living room where Grandma peeled apples for all of us. We heard stories of tending the chickens and Mother's pet lamb, shucking popcorn, and picking grapes and cherries. Grandpa sat with his feet propped on an old hassock. He wasn't actually tired; he would tease that he was protecting his treat stash inside the hassock. We all knew we weren't allowed to sneak from the candy and chocolate he kept in there. However, since my grandfather was of German descent, his favorite treat, which happened to be Limburger cheese, was also kept inside the hassock. This ruined my desire for the chocolate! We were happy with our apples and pennies.

I now have Grandma's glass piggybank full of her pennies she handled at one time. I don't know what happened to her milk glass hen, but I have a glass chicken dish of my own so I can treat my grandchildren in the same loving way when God so blesses. For now, I've placed four pennies in my chicken, and when I see the pennies in that chicken and wear Grandma's butterfly pin, I feel blessed, well thought of, and loved by God.

– Ella Forner

73

Several years ago when Mrs. Cindy Schaap challenged us to get our own "God loves me" sign, I chose cardinals and chickadees. Being somewhat of an insecure person, I decided I needed all the signs I could get, so through the years I've added more, such as butterflies and daisies. Recently, I added bunny rabbits to the list, and I have been so sweetly blessed by seeing them at the most important times that I **needed** a sign!

One morning as I was driving to the library, a rabbit was sitting in a yard on a side street, nibbling away, and when I came back by a few minutes later, he was still there and didn't even hop away when I rolled down my window and thanked God for the sign and told Him I loved Him too.

Recently, while I was going to a dollar store with our youngest daughter Emily to pick up some things for another of our children who was being hospitalized, we noticed a baby bunny nibbling plants in the middle of a flower and shrub arrangement in front of the store! It's extra-special to see your sign(s) in such unexpected and unusual places!

God is just so sweet to manifest Himself and His love toward us in such opportune ways and places if we will just ask Him to. I challenge you to get your own sign. It will draw you closer to your Heavenly Father! I promise!

– Jan Bingaman

74

Our family went on vacation to the Mount Baker, Washington, area where we saw many beautiful sights. One day my oldest daughter Brianna and I were going to have some time together just going out on same-day hikes in the vicinity. We took the vehicle and headed up the south side of the mountains to go into the national forest and pick which hikes we might like the best. As we were ascending, we both asked God to let us see something unusual and amazing while we were on the trip—thinking we might come across some awe-inspiring waterfall, stream, or field of breathtaking wildflowers.

As we were driving along an old logging road, suddenly we saw something cross in front of the vehicle. We came to a complete stop and just looked at each other in absolute unbelief. A beaver, pulling a small log, came to a complete stop and stared right back at us as if to say, "What? You've never seen a beaver before?"

As he sat in the roadway, we both told the Lord "Thank You!" and then tried to take a picture to get proof that it had happened. Mr. Beaver chose that moment to continue on toward his destination. We both laughed hysterically because we knew that the rest of the family would never buy our tale, but we have each other as a witness and a wonderful God Who gave us just what we had asked for!

– K'arin Hanson

75

In Colorado we have 54 mountain peaks that are over 14,000 feet. Climbing "fourteeners" is a popular sport. Although I do not consider myself to be in great shape for mountain climbing, I do have a great desire. I climbed my first fourteener with our two youngest boys just before my son David went off to college. I learned many lessons on that climb, and it will always be a special memory for each of us.

My second fourteener will be remembered with much excitement for the unique way God showed Himself to Me! My hiking buddy and I drove to the town nearest the trailhead for

Mount Bierstadt. Once we were settled into our hotel room, we decided to check out the trailhead so we would know exactly where we were going the next morning. The weather was not looking good, and the fog was rolling in. By the time we reached the parking lot, visibility was poor. It took us a while to find the trailhead, and then we began to make our way back to town. As we were slowly driving down the pass, we had to stop as two large animals passed right in front of us. We sat there, eyes wide with excitement and mouths too shocked to speak, as a mother moose and her baby crossed the road. We couldn't believe what we were seeing, so when we got to the bottom of the pass, we asked a road worker if there were moose in the area.

"Yes," she said, "a mother moose and her baby live up here, but they are rarely seen." God knew how much we would rejoice over letting us see this creation of His, and He gave us a rare gift. We were concerned that weather might keep us from making the climb or seeing much of a view from the summit. We asked God for a clear day and should not have been surprised when we walked out of our hotel room before 5:00 a.m. to clear skies. As we began to hike, the trail descended into a valley before beginning to climb. The sun was coming up as we came out of the valley, and the fog was still lying in the valley. It was so beautiful.

I live in Woodland Park, and it is called "the city above the clouds." God knows my favorite scene is when we have sunshine and blue skies in Woodland Park, but the area where Mount Bierstadt is located usually has overcast weather. I love to see the clouds lying in and around the mountains as we drive down the pass.

I kept telling my hiking buddy that I hoped the fog would still be there when we reached the summit so we could look down on it from the top. She kept telling me that if I didn't hike any faster, the sun would burn it all off before I reached the top. I did my best, but as I got closer and closer to the summit, the sun had done its job and burnt off the fog in the valley. Nevertheless, it was beautiful to watch the sun shine down on the western slope. What we thought to be a little town in the distance was actually the parking lot where our vehicle was parked and was now joined with many other vehicles of hikers making their way to the summit.

Mount Bierstadt is very rocky as you reach the summit and a little tricky to maneuver. We finally made it to the top, and I could not believe my eyes. The entire eastern slope was socked in with fog! Here we sat at 14,060 feet looking down on the clouds. Other mountain peaks were visible above the clouds, and it was a spectacular view. It was definitely a "specific act of God." He knows how much I love to be above the clouds and still have both feet on the ground. He knows I need the reminder that when my days are "cloudy," the Son is still shining up above. He showed Himself to me in a most unique way, and I felt so loved.

This was a mountaintop experience that I will never forget, but I don't want to just end there because God shows His love to me in many ways. I also think it is just as unique when He gives me what I need from His Word. It is a specific act of God each day that He has just what I need from His Word. How does He know with what I will be struggling on the day that I'm reading a certain passage? It simply confirms to me that my

Bible is a living Book from a loving God. I still have a lot to learn about recognizing the ways God shows His love to me, but it's been a great adventure so far.

– Robin Parton

76

January 16, 2005, started as a regular day. My devotions in the morning were a sweet time of fellowship with my Lord. I sent my husband off to work as usual. As I drove to my hair appointment, my cell phone rang. That phone call was the beginning of this story.

The hospital called to tell me my mom had been in an auto accident. My youngest sister Mary had been driving her to a doctor's appointment. The weather was bad; and wet, heavy snow had made the roads wet and slushy. My sister lost control of her van and overturned into the ditch. She, her husband, and two children were uninjured—not even a scratch. My mother was hanging upside down, suspended in her seatbelt. She was not breathing, and I personally believe she died at that moment.

Rescue workers started all the life-saving techniques and transported her to the hospital. After being put on a ventilator, she was transferred to Marquette, a much bigger and more up-to-date hospital. It was a long drive.

There she lay for four days on life support. There was no response—only machines breathing for her and keeping her heart beating. Once our large family arrived from around the country, a decision had to be made. Our father and all eight children made the decision to allow Mom to go in peace. It was a heartbreaking tragedy to lose our mom this way. She had been on dialysis for five years. God knew it was her time to join Him. No more suffering. The joy she must have with Jesus now!

Five years earlier while on what we thought was her deathbed, our pastor, Paul Williams, led her to the Lord. Thankfully, she had survived that episode. As the doctors and nurses turned off the ventilator, we gathered around her bedside. My unsaved siblings allowed me to pray and to lead in singing "Amazing Grace." It was a blessing to do this one last thing for Mom. Praise God, I know she is in Heaven, and I will see her again someday.

Now for the rest of the story…In May 2006 our son-in-law and daughter, Nick and Beth Watt, left for New Zealand, their new home as missionaries. New Zealand is 27 hours by air from our home in the U.P. of Michigan. We live a good life, but finances are not in abundance. God has always supplied our every need and many of our wants. Praise God we can trust Him to take care of us. "Where will we ever get the money to travel to New Zealand?" I wondered.

God knew my heart and my daughter's heart. I had casually mentioned to my brother that I would like to go to New Zealand after a year or so. "I am trusting God to supply the need," I said.

Because of the accident with my sister's driving and my mother's death, my sister's insurance company paid a settlement to Dad. No one in the family pursued this course of action; the insurance company wanted to be finished with the episode and not have problems. My dad did not want or need the money. He instead chose to divide the money between his eight children. Praise God! He did provide the money I needed so I could fly to New Zealand and visit my daughter. My mother never understood our lifestyle after our salvation, but now she does! God is so good!

One year after my daughter left for New Zealand, through God's provision and perfect timing, I had the unspeakable joy of hugging my daughter on her mission field. With tears of bittersweet joy, we were able to spend her first Mother's Day on the mission field—missing my mom (and her grandma) but rejoicing in the unique gift from God. Just to show me how much He loves me, God allowed me to lead a lady in her 80s to the Lord while I was in New Zealand. My mom had just turned 80 at the time of her death. God is so great!

God allows joy and tears. Praise God He always knows exactly what we need in our lives. We may not understand the trials we must face, but He knows how everything will work out. He knows the whole story. He turned my mourning into joy. *"Thou hast turned for me my mourning into dancing; thou hast put off my sackcloth, and girded me with gladness."* (Psalm 30:11)

– Cindy Johnson

77

I love flowers—all types of flowers, but especially bright, cheerful flowers. A few years ago we did some landscaping in our front yard. I prefer flowers that do not require a lot of maintenance and also flowers that bloom all summer long. I had seen stella dora lilies in nearby yards and loved their bright yellow-gold color and the fact that they bloomed all summer, so I decided to plant a bed of stella dora lilies in my front yard. They bloomed beautifully, and I was so excited.

However, near the end of June the plants were flowerless... and remained so the rest of the season. I was disappointed, but I thought, "Maybe it's because this is their first year and the transplanting was traumatic for the plants."

The following two years the same thing happened. I had beautiful blooms in June and that was it. I would drive by other yards and see their beautiful stella dora blooms and drive home to green, flowerless plants. I asked other people for suggestions, but I was doing the things they said—watering them faithfully, fertilizing, keeping them thinned, etc.

Last summer as I was getting ready for work one day, I prayed for a friend who was going through a really tough time. We had talked, and she had done all she could do concerning the situation. The Lord had to do the rest. After I prayed for her, I said, "Lord, I sure would like to see You in a special way today." My heart was heavy for my friend, and I just wanted a little personal touch from God to reassure me regarding this situation.

I walked out my front door and stopped dead in my tracks. There, right in front of me, was *one* stella dora lily in full bloom. I walked to the flower bed, knelt down, and looked at it. With tears I said, "Jesus, I see You, and I love You too!" No more stella dora lilies bloomed in my yard the rest of the summer. I knew God had caused that one lily to bloom just for me on that day to give me some special encouragement. Over the next few months, God did some miraculous works in the life of my friend, giving me even more assurance that He had told that lily to bloom on that particular morning just for me!

– Jane Grafton

78

*I*t does seem to me that God uses flowers to show love to me in a special way. One day this past summer I seemed to particularly need a touch from God. I laughed to myself and thought, "Well, it won't be one stella dora lily blooming like last year because the whole bed is in full bloom right now."

I was shocked when I walked out my front door that morning. I happened to glance to the right, and at the end of my bed of hostas was **one** tiger lily grown tall and in full bloom. I laughed out loud. It looked like someone had very carefully planted that lily at the end of the bed! We had done landscaping in our front yard a few years ago because of some work we had done on our basement. The only thing I can figure is that the tiger lily must have gotten buried deep in the ground with all the digging, and it took three years to get back up out of the soil!

Recently I have been asking God for some really big things. These are not personal things for me, but some prayers I want to see answered that will make a difference for eternity. I have sometimes doubted when I pray because my requests seem so impossible.

However, a few days ago when I arrived home from work, I got out of my car and was absolutely beside myself at the sight in my yard. A pink day lily was growing up in the midst of another bed of hostas in front of our house (on the side opposite of the tiger lily.) Then I looked and saw more day lilies shooting up through the ground. We had not had any day lilies since landscaping three years ago. As these "miracle" lilies have come into full bloom, it's as if the Lord is telling me, "I hear your prayers, and just as it took three years for these lilies to come up out of the ground, I knew where they were all the time; in My own time I had them spring forth...in time to let you know I'm hearing your prayers."

– Jane Grafton

79

In January of 2000 I was experiencing some heart problems. My cardiologist diagnosed a leaky mitral valve that possibly would need to be repaired or replaced. I went through all the tests leading up to surgery. Many people prayed for me and my condition, and as a result, God answered prayer. The doctor said I would not need surgery, but I would have to take some prescription medicines.

We are part of a Christian organization that is not an insurance company but helps pay our medical bills; it offers no assistance with prescriptions. Many times my cardiologist and family doctor have given me free samples of some of my prescription medicine. Every time I leave the doctor's office with my little brown sack of samples, I feel like a little girl leaving a candy store with the biggest grin on her face. Yes, I'm thrilled that the doctor did that for me, but most of all, I feel God loves me and He has given me a big hug.

Something happened on December 26, 2006, that I will never forget. Our family doctor no longer gets samples of one of my prescription drugs. It was a week before Christmas, I had run out of that particular pill, and I felt I had more important things on which to spend our money. I had taken the prescription to the pharmacy a couple of days before but had not picked it up.

My husband and I were at a Christmas party, and I wasn't feeling well. I thought to myself, "I should have gotten my pills at the pharmacy." I knew the next morning was our Sunday school Christmas program and I would be busy. When we left the party, I called a lady from our church and asked if she would call the pharmacy to see if it was still open. She called me back and said there was no answer. My husband and I drove to the pharmacy to see if they had any Sunday hours. They didn't open until 10:00 a.m., and I knew I would have to be at the church before then.

I called a doctor who was a former neighbor and asked him if he happened to have a couple of the pills I needed to get me through the weekend. He paused for a moment and then said, "As a matter of fact, I do. I'm not home right now, but if you go by my house, there is a brown sack on my porch with the medicine you need. There's enough for the next three months."

To God be the glory! God does love me, and He cares about me. As my husband went to the porch that wintery night and picked up the little brown sack contained medicine for me, I once again felt like a little girl leaving a candy store with a big grin on her face. Yes, God loves me!

– Marcia Schearer

80

The week after Marlene Evans went to Heaven, I helped Loretta Walker clean the Evans's house. Other than that, I had not been at the Evans's house since the day Mrs. Evans went to Heaven. A month or so after her Homegoing, Joy Ryder, their missionary daughter, asked me to go to the Evans's house to pick up some items for her. To get them, I had to go into the downstairs where Mrs. Evans had stayed in her final days until her Homegoing. As I walked in, memories flooded my mind.

Tears began to come to my eyes, but I held them back. I remembered the Sunday when Pastor and Mrs. Schaap came to the house after the Sunday morning service to see Mrs. Evans. While they were in her room, Mrs. Evans went to Heaven. My heart was knit to Mrs. Schaap as I watched her come to the living room and talk to everyone who was there that day. I was sitting on a recliner behind the door. I tried to hold back my tears but couldn't. I was trying to stay out of the way since everyone else in the room had worked for her much longer than I had. I still remember so vividly how after Mrs. Schaap talked to everyone else, she came over to where I was sitting and gave me a hug. I do not remember exactly what was said, but I remember feeling so loved by her.

Mrs. Evans was widely known for her love of redbirds. She even wrote a book entitled *Redbirds and Rubies and Rainbows.* As I left the Evans's house after doing my errand, out from a bush flew a redbird! I know Mrs. Evans had seen many redbirds at her house, but I do not ever remember seeing one anytime I was there. I could not keep the tears from coming. I cried all the way back to Hyles-Anderson College where I work. I somehow felt that God and Mrs. Evans caused that redbird to be there just for me. I felt like both of them were saying, "Gina, I love you."   – Gina Eyer

81

I have no doubt that God loves me very much. He shows His love to me every day in so many different ways. One way has to do with eagles. My mom's favorite verse was Isaiah 40:31, which says, *"But they that wait upon the LORD shall renew their strength; they shall mount up with wings as eagles; they shall run, and not be weary; and they shall walk, and not faint."* In March of 2002 my mom went home to be with the Lord, and I have missed her so much. Whenever I see an eagle, it reminds me of my mom, her love for the Lord, and God's goodness to me in giving me such a wonderful mother.

Living in the Northwest, I see eagles occasionally, but nothing like I did on Tuesday, July 10, 2007. My husband and I went fishing with our oldest son Tim and a family from our church. We went to Neah Bay, Washington, which is on the northwest point of the Washington peninsula. It is strictly a fishing place, not a shopping place. We got up at 5:00 a.m. so we could get ready, have breakfast, and be on the boat by 6:15 a.m.

About 5:05 I began to wonder what in the world I was doing up at that hour just to go fishing! We left our friends' trailer to go to the dock and passed a small beach. The sun was up, it was already a beautiful day, and I saw one of the most wonderful sights I have ever seen. On the beach sat four huge eagles having breakfast, flying around, and seemingly just soaking up the sun. I watched them so much I was worried I might walk right off the walkway into the water! During the six hours we were out fishing, we saw three more eagles in different places. Two of the eagles were going after sea gulls and were then chased by dozens of gulls. I was awestruck at the sight and sound of all those birds!

After cleaning up and getting back to the campsite, I looked up and saw yet another eagle circling above our camping area. I just sat there and thanked God for giving me such a great day. God not only gave me many reminders of my mom that day, but He also seemed to speak to my heart and say, "I surely do love you!"   – Darlene Minge

82

With great anticipation I look forward to the 2007 Christian Womanhood Spectacular, "O Taste and See That the Lord Is Good!" Prior to this penning, I had looked forward to the sharing of all the ways God shows ladies around the country that He loves them. Being a rather private person, sharing what I perceive as God showing His love toward me had not really entered my mind. Then one quiet afternoon I received a phone call from a friend and a leader in the ministry in which we serve together. With much persuasiveness, she convinced me to share this personal part of my life.

When I was growing up, my mother taught me many important attributes. I wholeheartedly believe that two of these attributes have created an avenue for the Lord to show me He loves me. The first attribute is to say, "Yes." When "they" call, you say "yes." In our Christian circles, the calls for help and assistance will come, and when they do, the answer to say is "Yes!" The second attribute is to **give**. Give your time, give your help, give your money—whatever the need is, just give. While I was growing up, money was never in excess, but somehow everyone who knew us thought we were wealthy. It wasn't until adulthood that my mother and I concluded that generosity was often mistaken for wealth.

Remarkably, I cannot remember my mother ever telling anyone "No." Many times she was one of the first ones called. Following in her footsteps in this area has truly allowed God to show me He loves me!

Eleven years ago while attending Hyles-Anderson College, I was called upon by Hylander Wives (the student wives organization) to make meals for fellow college wives who had had babies or surgeries. On one such occasion, the leader calling me apologized profusely for contacting me every time. She explained that my last name was at the end of the alphabet and that she had called everyone above me and was unable to fill a particular need.

On that particular day, I shared something with her that only my husband, my mother, and the Lord knew. I told her to call me every time and never to apologize. As crazy as it might sound, every time I made a meal for someone, God would send me money—usually within 48 hours.

I was afraid that day when I shared the secret that God and I had shared for over a year, that the money would stop coming. But quite the contrary has happened. For nearly 12 years, every time I provide a meal for someone, the Lord shows me His love by sending money. There has never been an exception. The money comes from such unusual places that I know that it has been sent from the Lord.

On one occasion, I received a survey in the mail with two 20 dollar bills paperclipped to it. Another day a local pizza chain randomly called my home and asked me to participate in a focus group to give my opinion of their pizza. They gave me $75 cash. Once my husband switched employers, and he called his main office to inquire about getting paid for two unused vacation days. They informed him that they did not owe him for two days, but for two weeks!

Several weeks ago a friend in our church stopped me in our lobby on a Wednesday night and asked me to make a meal for someone who was having surgery in a few days. I, of course, agreed. I took my son to the third-floor nursery, came back to the first floor, and walked through the auditorium to my seat. A lady in our church approached me. She opened a manilla envelope and pulled out a piece of computer paper with printing on it. She asked me if this was my husband and our current address. Indeed it was. The paper was a printout from

IndianaUnclaimed.com. We had a little over $200 sitting in an unclaimed account.

There is no way I could possibly list every occurrence. I do know that the one common denominator is that the money God sent was always preceded by my providing a meal for someone in need. I say this respectfully, but it has almost become comical in our home. If a need arises—as they do in all homes—my husband will often say, "Isn't there anyone for whom you can make a meal?"

A little over a year ago, four weeks before Christmas, we received a newly assessed and rather unexpected property tax bill for around $1,000. With Christmas just a few weeks away, that bill worried me. My husband very seriously and calmly stated, "Isn't there anyone you can make a meal for?"

I clearly remember telling my husband, "This is going to take more than a meal!" God had never failed to show His love toward me in the past, but then I had never made a meal with the expectation of God's fulfilling "His end of the bargain."

A few days later the son of one of our church shut-ins unexpectedly passed away, and I was called upon to help provide the food for the funeral. As I recall, about a week later I was attending a Christmas luncheon for a ministry in which I serve when my cell phone rang. I checked the caller ID and saw that it was my husband. I excused myself to the restaurant foyer and took the call.

My husband stated he had just gotten the mail and that we had received a Christmas card. My husband was rather choked up but was able to say that the card had a check in it.

I instantly recalled the $1,000 tax bill and wondered if this was how God was going to take care of it. My husband, with a shaken voice, said, "Jeanie, the check's not for a thousand dollars; it's for **ten** thousand dollars!"

I was stunned, speechless, and convicted. God had sent a clear message, "I love you even when you doubt Me." To this day, there has never been a time when I have provided a meal for someone that God has not shown in a very definite way that He loves me.

For some it's butterflies or deer or pennies or redbirds, but for me, God has chosen money. Perhaps that is why I love Matthew 6:21, *"For where your treasure is, there will your heart be also."* Surely every time the Lord sends me *"treasure,"* I must be in His heart also.   – Jeanie Winget

$$\mathscr{8}\mathscr{3}$$

$\mathscr{I}$remember Mrs. Marlene Evans always saying, "Look for the rainbows in life" or "I saw a red cardinal today" or how the trees, deer or blue herons always told her God loved her. I have adhered to that teaching and told my family the same things.

"Oh, there's a redbird, Mom," Ruthie would say.

"I don't see it," I would say. "God must love you today!"

Blue herons became my favorite, and I would scour every pond I saw just looking for a sign and then jumping for joy in my heart and sometimes even in the car. I'm sure my family thought I was nuts!

The year 2007 brought a different kind of love from God. At age 50, I thought we had come through life soaring above the clouds. I knew life would never be perfect, but this age brought promises of a normal life. Two of our children were now married, and only one child remained at home. It was soon to be just the two of us!

January 2007 my husband boldly stated, "This is going to be a great year, Honey. I can feel it." We owned our own print shop where our youngest daughter and married son also worked. Those cold January days were very busy and long. My husband Dan was the hardest worker I had ever known. Our family all helped and worked alongside.

But I could tell my husband's health was failing. Shortness of breath, chest pains, and other pain came upon him, but there was no time to go to the doctor, nor was there extra money for hospital tests. I tried to get him to go, but in his mind, he was caring for his family. I then asked God, begging Him again and again.

God had been listening, and in October 2006 He began His work in our lives. My husband's dad had gone to Heaven suddenly from the complications with his heart and diabetes. He left behind a sugar testing kit, and Dan's mother sent it home with us. Jokingly, my husband took a sugar test and saw it was high. God planted a seed in his mind to beware. God loved him, and God loved me.

One night in January 2007, my husband came home chilled and shaking. His eyes and face looked white and puffy. He fell into bed, and I gave him some medicine. I prayed, "God, he will not go to the doctor unless You tell him." I couldn't sleep and told our daughter to pray for Daddy. "He is very sick."

It may sound strange, but "something" told me not to sleep

that night and to pack some items to stay at the hospital. I know now that "something" was God. At 2:00 a.m. my husband was sitting on the side of the bed unable to walk well and said, "I am ready to go to the hospital." We were having a small snowstorm as I drove. I knew God loved me.

God brought the best doctors and nurses to us, and we later learned that my husband needed a five-way bypass (two arteries were completely blocked). He was also fighting a very high sugar count and had insulin-dependent diabetes.

I was able to stay night and day with my husband. God knew that nothing else mattered. God was there days ahead. The doctors were afraid Dan might have a heart attack before the surgery and moved him to ICU.

God loved us! My husband was so brave and had a sense of humor through all of this. God loved us through others too. Family from out of town came for the surgery; friends from church brought notes of encouragement, gifts—exactly when we had a need for food, medicine, personal comfort items, and money; friends came just to sit with me the day of the surgery. God loved me through a hug from a friend, a prayer from Brother Johnny Colsten, the side-splitting laugher of Brother Eddie Lapina, and a kind call from our pastor about the surgery. God loved me the night before surgery as I sat alone in the waiting room crying out to Him, then reading His word for comfort. He gave me physical strength the next day—even without sleep.

As time passed and each day brought new things, I prepared for my husband to come home. Someone said, "He may need a recliner to sleep in and be comfortable." I knew what we had wouldn't work, but I had no money to get a new chair. That very evening my sister and her husband gave me just enough money, along with the other monetary gifts we had received, to be able to purchase a nice chair at just the right price! God loved me!

After coming home one evening from the hospital, I was lying on our bed and knew our worn-out mattress and bed would be so uncomfortable to him while recuperating. I felt selfish but asked God for a new bed. The next morning I laughingly told my daughter about my prayer. That very afternoon I received a call from my mother-in-law telling me she had a queen bed with new mattresses if I wanted them for a spare bedroom. God loved me!

God used our family. Our son and his wife worked many long hours at our shop—tired but not complaining. My son-in-law and daughter helped them, cared for my rides, went out of town to get the bed and then set it up for us. Our youngest daughter worked at the print shop when she wished to sit at the hospital with her daddy. God loved me.

February came. God loved us and provided for our needs. Doctor appointments followed; we went through sugar highs and lows, but God gave me time to be with Dan.

In March a call came that my dad had suffered a heart attack and was not expected to live. We drove three hours to see Grandpa. God loved me because when we arrived he "came back," sat up in the hospital bed, told corny jokes, and laughed a lot. That night was the last time that my dad was himself.

My husband, who was still recovering, stayed as long as he could until his sister (a nurse) told him he had to get some rest. My dad continued to linger. My sister and I stayed by him a few nights at the hospital. One night I reminded him how I loved him and how Jesus loved him. "Remember how you accepted Jesus?" I asked. He squeezed my hand and simply said, "Uh huh." God loved him, and God loved me enough to give me that special time of assurance. God gave my husband strength to uphold me during those days. I felt so strong yet so weak.

God loved my 88-year-old mom and gave her strength to allow my dad's wishes to die naturally. I felt God sent an angel from hospice to help us let him go.

The funeral came, my sister's friends and church gave love, but I missed my church at this time. My brother-in-law came to me and said, "Your pastor has called several times to speak to you." I felt very loved because these calls were made during a very busy time for my pastor—the annual Pastors' School. Then as I admired the beautiful flowers, I noticed that two arrangements came from my church. God loved me.

My husband and I helped my mom move in with my sister and her family. As we were all sitting on my sister's screened-in porch, my husband brought the laptop to me and said, "Our son-in-law and daughter sent us something by email." I had to read the message twice to realize that they had put together a little poem informing us that we were going to become grandparents in October! What a precious gift from God!

Life finally got back to normal for us. In the month of June, our 21-year-old daughter was walking to the mailbox when a pit bull broke a chain and attacked her. My husband saw it and tackled the dog. Our daughter had painful scrapes and bites on her back and down her arm. She received 22 stitches. But God protected and cared for them both.

I still say that 2007 is a great year! I still look for redbirds and rainbows. Whether God sends you nature, shows you a special verse, provides needs through others, or lets you walk very quietly beside Him, God loves you.

Yesterday my daughter excitedly said, "Mom, come here quick."

"What?" I asked.

"There's a white heron in the pond!"

God loves me!

– Nancy Musser

84

Daily in big and small ways, the Lord shows His love for me, but some ways are more unique and definitely more memorable! While growing up in a Christian home, I always knew of God's love, but the following story is a specific act of God where He showed His love for me.

In 1981 during the final service at a summer camp, I surrendered to full-time Christian service, and I knew the Lord wanted me to attend Hyles-Anderson College. A few years later my dad (then 40 years old) was medically retired, and my hopes of attending college were dimmed. Many attempts were made to obtain medical retirement benefits, and during my senior year of high school, medical benefits were once again denied. Yet another letdown, but I knew the Lord had called me to Hyles-Anderson College. I was just going to trust Him to work it out and to bring it to pass. *Trusting* was easier said than done because summer 1988 was swiftly passing, and I had no idea how I was going to get to Hyles-Anderson in just a few short weeks!

The first Sunday in August came, and during the morning service, a lady sang "God Will Take Care of You." While she was singing, I felt like I was the only person in the auditorium and the Lord was telling me that **He would** take care of me and my needs. Once the invitation started, I raced to the altar and asked the Lord to forgive me of my doubt and worry. Then I asked Him for one more thing—$1,000! I figured that amount would help me get to college and get started, but if He wanted to give me more, I let Him know that would be just fine. I also told the Lord that I was not telling anyone else about this request because I was going to trust Him to take care of this need. When I got off my knees, I had such peace mixed with giddiness, but I knew without a doubt that I was headed to Hyles-Anderson College.

Later that week I was at church, and my pastor asked if I would be home later that evening because he needed to bring something by. When he came, he met with my parents, and then they called me in. I sat down at the kitchen table, and my pastor began to speak. He proceeded to tell me that this "message" was not from him—but from the Lord—he was just God's messenger boy. He then handed me an envelope and told me that each Gospel tract inside represented a $100 bill. Of course, the envelope felt as if it contained hundreds of tracts! My heart was pounding as I opened the envelope and with a shaking hand, I slowly pulled out the stack of tracts. I began to count "1, 2, 3… (I knew that would cover my registration) 4, 5, 6, 7…

(that would take care of my first tuition payment) 8, 9…10!!" I bowed my head and began to cry tears of joy. My parents and my pastor were just a little shocked, so they began asking if I was okay. Through my tears I said, "The Lord is good," and then I began to tell them about the events of the preceding Sunday's service. We all started praising the Lord together.

At that very moment, for the first time, I felt very special to the Lord, and I knew that **He heard me** and more than anything **He loved me**. Opening Day 1988 at Hyles-Anderson College came, and I was there! My parents and I had no idea how we would make the next payments, but later I would come to realize that this $1,000 was just the first of many payments that would come from the Lord for my school bill. At the graduation service of 1993, I walked across the platform of First Baptist Church of Hammond, not owing a penny to Hyles-Anderson College, but knowing even more that the Lord loved me.   – Kay Souther

85

Secretly observing the magnificent heavens from a diminutive wrought-iron bench partially concealed beneath the long, groping arms of an ancient apple tree, I reclined there listening to the cadence of rolling thunder in the not-too-distant, murky sky. Undaunted by this loud crash of Heaven's cymbals in the symphony of nature's song, I waited with anticipation for the rhythmic chimes of the soft pattering I knew would soon engulf me. Even as I contemplated this audition of sound, the glowing moon became eclipsed by nebulous clouds. The wind began to stir, and the fragrance of an approaching shower saturated the air.

Filled with wonder and delight as that gentle summer rain began to fall, I lifted my face toward its warm caress. I let it wash over me, yielding unreservedly to its ardent embrace. As the tiny droplets kissed my cheeks and stroked my windswept hair, I closed my eyes and reflected on how much my Heavenly Father loves me. Like a sponge, I soaked up the pleasurable rain and then bathed in the awareness of God's affection.

Suddenly awakened from my reverie by a flash of brilliant illumination, I opened my eyes to see streaks of lightning dance across the mysterious sky. Although the lightning appeared ominous and oppressive, I never felt a moment's apprehension. Instead, I hugged my knees tightly to my chest, bowed my drenched head in tranquil reverence, and thanked God for the peace and serenity that only He can give in the midst of a storm.   – Taralynn Hooker

[a creative writing assignment for a Hyles-Anderson College class]

86

One of my favorite experiences that God used to demonstrate His love to me was traveling from the 2006 Spectacular. I was going straight from the Spectacular to meet my husband and son at the Dallas Airport for the Soul-Winning Clinic in Longview, Texas. We were trying to arrange our flights where we would arrive in Texas in the same general time frame. The Dallas Airport is very large, and I was a bit concerned about getting my luggage and meeting up with them. It all seemed a bit overwhelming to me. I had ordered my tickets earlier than I had ordered theirs, and I was so excited that our flights were going to arrive at exactly the same time so that we wouldn't have to wait on each other.

After the purchase, I had a scare. I thought I had done something wrong because the flight numbers on their tickets were the same as mine. It was then I realized that they left Pittsburgh Airport, then switched air planes at Midway Airport in Chicago, and we would be traveling to Dallas on the SAME plane! I had not asked the Lord for this gift—He just loves me so much that He wanted me to have the security of arriving in Dallas on the same plane as my husband and son. They were such a great help because they carried my luggage for me.

The most recent evidence that God loves me has been in the fact that I became very interested in perennial plants after organizing the landscaping at our church. I have also really been wanting mountain laurel for our property as it is indigenous to this region. I used my birthday money to purchase what I could, but it was just a drop in the bucket when you are wanting to "decorate" three acres.

Recently the Lord has been laying it on the people's heart to "share" their perennials with me, and I ended up with not one, but two mountain laurel plants. Because they are the state flower of Pennsylvania, It is illegal to dig them up unless they are on your property, so I had no idea how to get them! What a generous God we have!

– Mimi Redick

87

*I*t was one of the darkest days of my life. I was in a hospital room where my mother lay a few feet from me—just hours from her Homegoing. As I sat peering out the window at the raging snowstorm, I noticed a small tree loaded with birds. I watched in fascination as the birds struggled to hold on to the tree branches as the seemingly angry wind was determined to shake them out of the tree. The limbs were snapping up and down and sideways with such force that I just knew the birds had no chance of hanging on. But the little birds did hang on!

At that moment I saw the comparison of myself to the birds on that tree. Another type of storm was raging inside the hospital room where the wind of death had entered and was an unwelcome guest. Like the little birds, I too was struggling to gain the extra strength needed to hold on while my world was being shaken. As I watched the struggling birds, I thought of Matthew 10:31, where Jesus assures us that we are of more value than many sparrows. A calm came over me as I realized that if Jesus, in His infinite mercy, gives these birds the strength to hold on until the storm passes, how much more sufficient would His grace be toward me. I knew then that I didn't have to hold on; Jesus was there to hold tight to me until my storm passed.

Whenever I see birds perched side by side on the power lines like little soldiers standing guard, I am reminded of that day and how much Jesus loves me.

– Narcie Ferrell

88

Six years ago life was busy with rearing our five children and helping care for my mother. Up early, packing lunches, making breakfast, dressing, getting the children out the door on time, driving them to school, and then I would return home to clean up after the "tornado." By noon I needed to be at my mom's house to clean, fix meals, wash her hair, etc., because of her poor health. I'd take her and my brother's laundry with me, pick up my kids, go home, start supper, do laundry, and work on homework, etc. I would go to bed exhausted and wake up tired.

After hearing Mrs. Cindy Schaap speak at Metro Baptist Church and encourage the ladies to find a reminder that God loves us, I went looking to see how God was going to show me He loves me. It wasn't in scenic beauty or wildlife. It took quite a few weeks and came totally unexpected.

Another hurried morning, and there it was—I opened the dryer door—and discovered God loves me! In our little laundry room/half bath/dog bedroom, I was on my knees crying—He loves me! How? The dryer was empty! Having an empty dryer is as rare as seeing a giraffe in a household of seven! God knew I would need this.

A few months later my mom was hospitalized and would become a dialysis patient. I now needed to be at the dialysis center by 10:30 a.m. to take her home and care for her until 5:00 or 6:00 p.m. when my brother or sister could take over. In the midst of this, my husband and I were blessed with another baby. Yippee—more laundry!

My dryer was empty every time—just every time I needed. Mom went to Heaven two years ago. Before I was to take her dress to the funeral home, I brought it home to freshen it with a home dry-cleaning kit. God loves me! I opened the dryer and found it empty!

– Delores Letson

89

When I was a child, I was homeless for several years. We lived with other folks and made many memories. That homeless time has stayed with me; therefore, having a home seemed very important. A few years ago our family went through a transition time when we didn't have a motor home or a home. I was homeless once again.

We didn't have money to rent a house, and especially with being in evangelism, we needed to have a permanent residence that didn't cost too much. A friend allowed us to move into an unused warehouse. It had a couple of large rooms with a bathroom but no shower. I've always been the type to make the best of any situation, so I put rugs on the floor and made paths to the rooms for the children to have fun. They were encouraged to use the mattresses for trampolines, and they could ride their bicycles using the furniture for an obstacle course.

One day while my husband was out with the children having fun, I was feeling homeless. I looked around and evaluated my life in a negative way. I was 40 with no home or money to buy one, no shower in which to take a decent bath, no windows to look out, boxes piled all around, etc. I was having a great pity party and enjoying every minute of it.

I went away from the children and closed myself into a small closet. I sat on the floor in a corner and had a heart-to-heart chat with God. I remember so well the feeling that overwhelmed me sitting there in that closet. I wrapped my arms around my legs, and I felt God wrap His arms around me. I felt comforted as a still, small voice whispered in my ear, "I understand; I care. It's okay to hurt." The empty feeling I had as I entered the closet was replaced with a feeling of the fullness of God's love. God showed me that day that He loved me with a hug. It was just what I needed.

– Loretta Walker

90

On Tuesday and Wednesday of Pastors' School 2007, at First Baptist Church of Hammond, Indiana, I sat and listened to pastors' wives speak and was amazed at their faith as God had brought them through incredible and difficult times. Early Thursday morning as I was driving in to the church, a car unexpectedly and seemingly out-of-nowhere backed out of a driveway into the street, and I could not stop nor avoid hitting the car. The airbags deployed, and as I sat stunned in my car, my first thought was "This is not what I needed on such a busy Pastors' School day."

Then it hit me, "God loves me" to entrust me with a car accident for which He knew I would praise Him. I thanked Him for believing in me that I would rejoice in how much He loves and protects me every moment of the day. As my body started to feel the aches and pains of being in a car accident, I kept saying, "Thank You God that You love me so much. I hope You know how much I love and trust You."

–Kris Grafton

91

This summer I have had a very special time of knowing that God loves me. We had just finished traveling in 12 states in the course of 15 days of speaking at churches doing wild game nights. (My husband is a wild game outfitter.) We were able to see the Lord work and see over 150 souls saved. My husband and I then took a trip to South Africa with our boys who are five and six. This trip to Africa was for business as well as a trip for the family.

Truthfully, I was quite apprehensive about taking my two boys to South Africa due to diseases, water, and many other dangers I knew we would be encountering. I did all of my homework on getting the proper shots and the proper medical attention needed prior to our trip. We also heard lots of opinions about our proposed trip on which we were about to embark. My husband and I just turned it all over to the Lord, and our family prayed together about this matter for weeks prior to leaving the States.

For the sake of time, let's just say we had a few close encounters, but the Lord took care of us, and none of us got sick, bitten, diseased, or even hurt! We were able to be with Christian people in South Africa and share the Lord's blessings at the dinner table every night. Several people did not have a daily walk with the Lord, and they were able to hear of His goodness through our life stories.

From the time we left by plane in South Africa until the moment we touched down in Great Falls, Montana, it was 37 hours! That's no time change—actual hours! The touchdown was the moment when I felt God's arms around me and could almost hear Him say, "I'm here. I've had you in my care all the way." My husband looked over at me and saw tears flowing from my eyes. He asked what it was and if I was all right.

I just said they were happy tears, and to this day, it brings tears to my eyes every time I think of how much God loves me and my family. To have the Lord protect my family and to have that long of a safe and happy flight with two boys was such a blessing.   – Marsha Schearer

92

*I*n the summer of 1981 we drove our son Steven to Lansing, Michigan, to work in the ministry under Dr. Don Green, Parker Memorial Baptist Church, where we had previously attended. The pastor, a widower at the time, graciously provided his own bedroom for my husband and me while we were there. On their dresser I noticed an Avon collectable that was a white porcelain pair of cupped ladies' hands to use as a ring or coin holder.

Throughout my life I have admired lovely things but rarely

coveted something belonging to someone else. However, I was fascinated by and longed for this feminine piece which had belonged to his dear wife who was now in Heaven. Only the Lord knew of the desire in my heart as I never mentioned it to anyone.

Six months later while looking through some things left by my mother who went to Heaven in December of that year, I found, to my astonishment, the same white porcelain Avon collectable of the cupped hands! It was as if the Lord was saying to me, "It was all right to desire this, and because I love you, it will be a special memory always for you of your former pastor's wife and your own dear mother." My tears flowed freely as I clasped it to my heart. This unique item now has had a place on our own bedroom dresser since that time.

The hands also remind me of Dr. Jack Hyles' silent sermon on going to God in prayer with empty cupped hands so He can fill them with good of every kind to give to others. Yes, I know God loves me! *"Delight thyself also in the LORD; and he shall give thee the desires of thine heart."* (Psalm 37:4)

– Helen MacCormack

93

Today is July 19, and it has been a little over 2 months (56 days to be exact) since my husband boarded a plane heading for Hammond, Indiana, leaving me and our four children in order to check himself in to the RU home.

Yesterday afternoon, my six-year-old son and I drove our

van (that for whatever reason cannot go over 40 miles per hour) to one of our church member's dealership to have it looked at. I already had some inclination that the news would not be good. The service manager came out and asked me how long this had been going on, and I told him about five days. With a puzzled look on his face, he replied, "How you have made it this long is beyond me." He told us that the transmission had a broken valve, and he really couldn't do anything for us. "How far do you live from the dealership? Do you have a cell phone?" he asked.

Not knowing if we would make it home, we prayed and asked God to get us home safely.

While driving back home, the questions ran through my mind. "Do I dare drive this van to church? Will we even make it home in time for church? Do I call my husband? Do I call our preacher?" As the tears ran down my face, my son looked at me and told me not to cry. "Will Sunbeam make it home?" he asked.

"I don't know, Buddy. Let's just keep praying," I answered.

"Yep, we'll make it home!" Wow, to have the faith of a child. I dried my face, called my husband, and drove very slowly. We pulled into our driveway at 6:15, and I knew we would not make it for church. I remembered that Youth Conference was going on and thought, "Maybe it will be on the Web."

I hurried, fixed the fastest dinner ever, set a "dinner table" in front of the computer, and clicked the view button on the FBC Web site…nothing. All the screen said was something along the line of "For our registered delegates…." Trying to fight back the tears, I moved everything back to the dining area.

About 45 minutes later, I heard something coming from the computer. When I got to the screen, Brother Chris Tefft was preaching, and so was our pastor! I clicked the minimize button on both sites, and may I add, it is really hard to listen to and watch two preachers at the same time! Once our preacher finished, I closed that window and started listening to Brother Tefft. He called one of the tour groups to come and sing. The music started, and my eyes filled with tears. You see, when Donnie left, the kids and I claimed Psalm 62:7 as our family verse. *"In God is my salvation and my glory: The rock of my strength, and my refuge, is in God."* We also chose a family song— "Were It Not for Grace." Yes, you guessed it, the tour group was singing "our" song. The children came running into the room, and our daughter stood there with a look beyond words, and said, "Mama, they're singing our song!" I turned to her and said, "Yes, I know, Sissy, and guess what? God really knows how to tell us He is real, that He loves us, and that everything is going to be okay."

I really don't know what lies ahead for our family, but I do know that I serve a gracious and loving God, and as long as I am given His grace, we will be okay. He loves me!

– Jodi Busby

94

A few years ago I decided to let my reminder of God's love for me be a cardinal. My mama went to Heaven on January 24, 2005, and just four short weeks later on February 21, 2005, my daddy joined her. As you can imagine, 2005 was a very difficult year. However, the Lord blessed me with five siblings who also share the heartache. That first Christmas without my loved ones was a "doozie." I was trying so hard to get into the Christmas spirit. The fact that God had blessed us with two sons helped because they were only eight and ten at the time.

From year to year I keep my Christmas cards, and as a yearly ritual before I start decorating, I sit and look at the cards from previous Christmases. I found the last Christmas card Mama sent to me in 2003 when she was still healthy. Mama was so sick from her cancer in 2004 she wasn't able to send any cards. The Holy Spirit directed Mama's kind, loving hand to choose one **for me** in 2003 with a "heavenly" message, the picture was of a little angel holding a redbird!

The Lord has let me see a redbird many, many times, but none quite as special as finding this redbird card. In March of this year, I began going through a very difficult time. This difficulty was actually harder on me than my parents' Homegoing. I believe the Lord sustained me from a nervous breakdown. I went through many, many sleepless nights, cried uncontrollably, and then laughed uncontrollably. Some people thought I did have some kind of a breakdown.

Whatever the case, I never ended up in the "crazy house" or on any kind of medication. I got into my Bible more, prayed more, and for several weeks with my husband's help, I totally guarded myself from hearing or seeing anything negative. We screened all of our phone calls. I watched no television news. If I did watch anything on television, it was family videos or programs like Anne of Green Gables. I tried to do and not do all the things that my pastor and Dr. Jack Hyles had taught us.

On March 9 I stayed in my room. In between praying, Bible reading, note writing, listening to preaching tapes, etc., I had started to reread Brother Hyles' biography, *The Fundamental Man.* Dr. Jack Hyles was one of my greatest heroes. After reading for a while, I closed the book to try to rest. I began to weep about a particular heartbreak and couldn't sleep. So I picked up the biography and began to read again.

The very place I started to read pertained to how Brother Hyles, as a boy, loved the St. Louis **Cardinals**! I just about had a fit! That was the first time God had ever used the word "cardinal." To some, these instances may seem "coincidental," but I know they have been tailor-made by God—just for me!

– Martha Gauldin

95

I have always loved oversized yellow butterflies. The first time I heard Mrs. Cindy Schaap give testimony claiming specific objects to signify God's love for her, I was inspired to do the same. I have to be honest, for a solid year I looked relentlessly for God to show me His love via a mammoth yellow butterfly. That year I witnessed a grand total of one large yellow butterfly. Now truthfully, I knew God had to love me more than the summation of the times I had seen my personal sign! Hence, I concluded that I must assign a new symbol of God's love for me. I wanted the object I would elect to be something unique. I could never quite settle on any one thing.

I teach biology at Hammond Baptist High School, and when I was given a new classroom, I asked for permission to paint and decorate it. I was surprised and a bit bewildered when the Lord impressed on me the idea of using a beach theme. I had never been a fan of using shells, sand, and such in my decor. I brought in multiple glass jars and asked my students that when they traveled to bring back a bit of sand for the jars in our classroom. As of this writing, we have sand from the Gulf of Mexico, Florida, Texas, Virginia Beach, California, and even Normandy.

My husband and I revisited Whiting Beach, the place where our engagement pictures were made. I filled a small glass with sand and returned to the car while my husband conversed with a local fisherman. As I waited for him, I felt the sand. I began to ponder casually the mentionings of sand in the Bible. I remembered God's promise to Abraham: that his seed would be multiplied as the sand on the seashore. Another vague reference kept eluding me.

The very next morning as I was following the Bible reading schedule provided by Dr. Schaap, I turned to Psalm 139 to begin my reading for the day. When I read, *"How precious also are thy thoughts unto me, O God! how great is the sum of them! If I should count them, **they are more in number than the sand.**"*

I became overwhelmed with a sense of God's love for me like I had never before experienced. He showed me that He is consumed with me—obsessed with me! I grabbed the glass of sand from Whiting Beach and started to imagine how much sand could possibly be in all the earth. I started to think about all of the things that are made of sand. At this point, I was almost hysterical. This was it! God had finally showed me what

He wanted my reminder of His love for me to be.

That day I began each of my classes by placing the amount of sand I could scoop with my fingernail on each desk. I asked my students to start counting the grains of sand. After about a minute, everyone realized that this was a very difficult task. As I was in the middle of my first-hour class giving this lesson, the Holy Spirit suddenly opened my eyes to all of the decor that was placed around my classroom—jars of sand, picture after picture of sand, blown-glass objects made from sand. I felt a second, overwhelming rush of God's love as He depicted the reason for the idea He had given to me to decorate my classroom with a beach theme. Every day I had been walking into a room where God was personally telling me millions of times, "I love you," and I had not noticed.   – Emily Moffitt

96

Years ago I read an article in *Christian Womanhood* that told of a young lady finding a penny and how it reminded her that God loved her. I thought a penny was a wonderful reminder as I saw the words "In God we trust," and I started looking for pennies also. Little did I know how much looking for pennies would help in years to come.

I continued to find pennies in lots of places and always picked them up and put them in my pocket. I told people how sweet the Lord was to let me find them in unexpected places just when I needed them the most.

In 2003 my husband, Jerry Nelson, was diagnosed with

Mesothelioma (cancer from asbestos) and went home to be with the Lord after only five months. He had been healthy for most of his life. He was known in our church as "Abe Lincoln" as he was 6' 5", and he would dress up in an Abraham Lincoln costume for various patriotic celebrations over the years.

A week after he was gone, I went for my usual mile walk, and as I looked down, I saw a penny. It was so sweet to see Abe Lincoln, and believe it or not, I had never really let it register before that he was on all of those pennies! It was a double blessing now as my "Abe" was in Heaven, and I needed to "trust the Lord" even more. He has been faithful and so good to me.

About a year later I was taking my walk again and listening to the tape of my husband's funeral for the first time. As I was listening to our former pastor, Dr. Ed Johnson, preach, he mentioned how Jerry had such a servant's attitude and would dress as "Abe" at a moment's notice. I was becoming teary-eyed, and right then as I looked at the sidewalk, I saw some pennies. I picked them up, looked around, and saw more. I crossed the street, and next to the boulevard, a HUGE pile of pennies beckoned me! By this time I was starting to laugh and thought, "God, how sweet You are to let me find all of these pennies." As I continued to pick them up, I noticed even more glistening pennies scattered all over the street.

Three boys came riding by on their bikes and teasingly asked if I was looking for money.

"Yes," I said and continued to pick them up and fill my jacket pockets. Pennies were under parked cars, in the grass, and on the sidewalk!

The thought hit me, "Am I on Candid Camera???" I even

stopped to look around for a hidden camera. By this time I was laughing and having a great time. I think God has a wonderful sense of humor, and I finally got all of them picked up. It was a very emotional time to think how the Lord wanted just ME to find all of them to let me know He is there for me in everything. After washing them and putting them on a cutting board in rows to count them, I found God gave me 165 wonderful pennies, and I felt VERY loved. God is so good!

My grandchildren love to hear this story, and I love to tell it, BUT I still love to find just *one* penny.

– Barb Nelson

97

I had been diagnosed with breast cancer. I was taking chemotherapy and feeling very discouraged. I had no hope. One day I was walking down Sibley Street in Hammond, Indiana, and some young ladies stopped to talk with me. They introduced themselves and told me they were students at Hyles-Anderson College. They continued talking and asked me if I knew for sure I was on my way to Heaven. When I told them "No," they explained to me from the Bible how to trust Christ as my Saviour. I prayed with the girls and got saved. They then invited me to their church, First Baptist Church of Hammond, and after a few minutes they went on their way.

That gave me hope, but I still felt discouraged about my cancer. A few days later I decided to visit that big church located just a few blocks from my apartment. I had never been in such a big church nor seen so many people in church at one time! I was looking for a seat when a lady kindly asked me, "Do you need a seat?" I told her I did, and she invited me to sit down beside her. After I sat down she looked at me and smiled as she said, "My name is Jane Grafton. What is your name?"

"Tina Delphie," I answered. She explained that she taught an adult ladies' Sunday school class and invited me to visit. I began attending the Friendship Class taught by Mrs. Grafton. God had used those college girls, First Baptist Church of Hammond, Mrs. Grafton, and the Friendship Class to encourage me.

My cancer went into remission, but in December of 2006 I went to the doctor because of extreme back pain. He discovered that the cancer had metastasized to my liver. The doctor gave me no hope of recovery. It was an extremely discouraging time for me because I wanted to live. I did not want to talk of death and dying. I know I am on my way to Heaven, but I want to accomplish some things for the Lord. I want to live.

God knew I needed to feel His love. When I was at a very low point alone in the hospital, I heard a knock on my door. It was Mrs. Grafton! Once again, God showed His love to me! She brought me a gift, prayed with me, and assured me she would have the class pray for me. We talked about my cancer and visited a little while. When she left, I felt very loved by God and encouraged that He had sent my Sunday school teacher.

In the months following while I've been on chemotherapy and treatment, Mrs. Grafton and the Friendship Class have visited me, sent cards, clapped for me when I walk into Sunday school after a chemo treatment, and been thoughtful of me financially. Each act of love on their part has been a reminder to me that God loves me very, very much.

– Tina Delphie as told to Jane Grafton

98

I woke up to the sound of a sniff. "She's crying again," I thought. Still, I allowed the night to pass without letting her know I had noticed. She needed to have the catharsis of letting her emotions out. Sure enough in the morning, I saw her puffy eyes and the dark circles around them. It had been another painful night for her.

I was surprised by her cheerful words—so opposite of her countenance. With shining eyes, she chattered, "Do you know what I dreamed last night? I was *walking* by the seashore, and I could run! Oh, what a day that will be when I can walk again. I wish I could be in Heaven now.…"

In the name of serving the Lord and for the sake of the ministry, my sister's simple and greatest wish is to once again walk. She has a rare type of kidney disease which is described in a short paragraph in medical books. When she was diagnosed with Fanconi's Syndrome, the doctors gave us a hopeless look and a discouraging statement: "There's nothing we can do about it. It's still under research."

Fanconi's Syndrome—A rare type of kidney problem where the nutrients taken into the body are excreted out in the urine due to a deficient reabsorbing capacity of tubules. It leaves the patient emaciated, with brittle bones, in severe bone pain called osteomalacia, and osteoporosis. Eventually the spine collapses and the bones become prone to minute fractures.

At 35 years of age, my sister has shrunk to a tiny frame of an eight-year-old girl, with shriveled extremities and a pigeon chest. It's devastating for loved ones to see her that way after she was enjoying a flourishing career, about to start a family, so full of youthfulness, and happily serving the Lord.

You see, since she's my roommate, my best friend, and my sister, I know what's going on beyond what others can see. Behind the facade of smiles are tears and pain of a normal human being. Having the simple aspiration of once again walking, she simply wants to serve the Lord Whom she loves. Instead of seeking to be comforted, my sister seeks to comfort others.

Despite her physical limitations and the pain she endures with each inch of movement, she continues to counsel people—young and old, teaches chemistry and physics, directs dramatic plays, encourages tired missionaries, performs secretarial jobs in church (from doing accounting tasks, sending emails, making tracts, to editing the church bulletin). Our brother carries her around in his arms when she goes to work. Though the Fanconi's Syndrome has left her physically incapacitated, it has never crumbled her spirit.

The doctor teased her one time after a kidney ultrasound and said, "You have a factory defect."

"Well, God doesn't make mistakes," she countered.

The saddest part for both of us was leaving her when God called me to get out of my comfort zone and go to another country—the USA. A meshwork of emotions came into play.

Unanswered questions, separation anxiety, and the thought of her being left alone in her pain and helplessness was a great challenge.

Once again, my sister set out to be the comforter instead of the one seeking to be comforted. "Obey and submit to the Lord," was her reminder. "Go, let go, and let God" became my motto. I know God loves me and my sister enough to tell us, "Trust Me in this, okay?"

Now my sister can walk again—not on her feet—but through the use of her fingers. Through God's mysterious ways, He used His people here who are so generous and sensitive to see my sister's need. This past August I returned to the Philippines to take my sister a birthday present—a special chair that she can control and manipulate with her fingers! She can "walk" again. God has provided all our needs and has given us the desires of our heart in His time. *"Now unto him that is able to do exceeding abundantly above all that we ask or think, according to the power that worketh in us."* (Ephesians 3:20)

– Nessah G. Jurao

99

One cold Saturday morning in November, we woke up and discovered that we had no heat or hot water in our house. My husband was out of town, and I had three very sick little girls. The company that delivers our fuel oil and maintains our furnace and water heater were backed up, couldn't come for a while, and wanted cash on the spot. With my husband gone, I knew I wouldn't have enough cash to pay them for parts and labor.

I called other companies to see what they could do, but no one would help me. Although the furnace was only a year old, I learned that due to a technicality, it was no longer under warranty. I called my husband, and he said not to worry about the bill; we would get it paid. I called our furnace company and told them to come when they could.

My sister wanted us to come and stay with her, and other people in the church offered us a place to stay as well, but I was afraid that I would miss the furnace repairman. We lived with no heat or water through Saturday and Sunday, and on Monday, the company called to say that a repairman could be there sometime within the next couple of days. I tried to tell them how sick my little girls were, and they were getting worse with no heat in the house. The message was still the same: "A repairman will be there as soon as he can." Life without heat and hot water for days and making my girls stay by the portable heater in the living room was getting a little rough. I had been asking God to intervene and help us with this problem, but now I began to beg and plead for Him to help us.

My sister came by on Wednesday to help out while we were still waiting for the repairman to come. My doorbell rang, and everyone was so excited. I opened the door, and a man with no uniform said, "I heard you were having problems with your furnace, and I am here to help you. Open the garage door so I can get to work."

It was like he had been in our garage before because he knew right where everything was. He went straight to the location of the circuit breaker panel (behind a door) and then went to the furnace and began working. He had been there for a while when my phone rang. The oil company was calling to say that they had subcontracted my job, and the repairman had been delayed.

I interrupted the caller and said, "There's someone here right now!"

"He's not with us," the company responded.

I put them on hold, walked to the garage, and asked the repairman if he was with my company. He said, "No," and I asked, "Who are you with?"

"I can't tell you," he said, "but tell your company not to come; it's taken care of."

I didn't know what to think. I ran up the stairs to tell my sister, and we were crying and praising God. I told my company not to worry about coming. I looked out the window and noticed "Wheaton Oil" on the side of the white van the repair-man was driving. No phone number was listed. I started to feel "strange" about the situation, but I was so happy that someone had finally come to help.

After he finished working on our furnace, he showed me exactly what he had done and made sure it was working prop-erly. I asked, "How much do I owe you?" knowing I had noth-ing to give him.

"Nothing. I heard that someone needed help, and it was the right thing to do," he simply said. "Pay me back by doing some-thing nice for someone else."

I bowed my head and started to cry and thanked God for helping me. When I looked up, the man was gone. I ran in the house and asked my sister if she had seen his van leave, and she said "No." My little girls were standing in the doorway crying and saying, "Thank you!"

I never got the man's name, but I know God sent me an "angel unawares" to help me. I will never forget that day as long as I live. God knew exactly what I needed, and He met my need above and beyond what I could have imagined. Later that day my sister looked in the phone book and could not find the name or a phone number for "Wheaton Oil." God truly does love me!

– Denise Baker

100

My dad was diagnosed with cancer two years ago. He had been on the prayer list at church for salvation for many years, but once he got sick the prayers were constant. He had surgery at the end of May in 2007 to have the cancer removed. His recovery was slow, but he finally moved closer to his home and was seemingly on the mend.

On Thursday June 21, I was at our church's very first ladies' prayer meeting. As I thanked the Lord for His longsuffering in keeping my dad around long enough that he might be saved, I could not know that he was slipping away at that very minute.

When the prayer meeting was over, I checked my cell phone messages and learned that my dad had been sent to the hospital. I was shocked to learn he was on life support. I took the first flight I could take on Friday morning, was met at the airport by my sister, and we drove five hours to the hospital. We prayed and prayed, hoping we could talk to him and make sure we could see him again someday in Heaven. Dad never responded in any way, and he passed away on Saturday.

Monday our uncle found my dad's old Army footlocker. He brought it over, thinking we might want to have it, but neither he nor any of us had any idea how much. Inside we found many pictures, letters, papers, and a little black Gideon's New Testament. I turned to the inside back cover where each Testament includes a place to sign and date under the words, "My Decision to Receive Christ as my Saviour." Signed in his own handwriting was Dad's name, Bob Hawley, and the date was October 11, 1961. In the front of the Bible on the presentation page, Dad had written his name, the same date, and the words "Army Draft." He had received the Testament on the same day he entered the Army *and* the Lord's Army. What a treasure! We had only two days of not knowing, and God answered our prayers. He could have made us wait years until we found it, but God is good and gave us a wonderful sign of His love.   – Nicolle Madkour

101

God showed me He loved me when He let me sleep a little extra one day. I had a great burden for my teenage son, and God had been waking me every morning between 3:00 and 3:30 a.m. to pray for him. I told God whatever time He woke me I would get up and pray. After several nights of not much sleep and being very tired, I prayed before I went to sleep. Once again I told God that I would get up and pray whatever time He awakened me. I then added in a sort of kidding (but not really) way, "…but I'm soooooo tired, and it would be really nice if You let me sleep just a bit longer." The next morning he woke me up at 4:59 a.m., only one minute before my alarm would go off!

———

God showed me He loved me when He let my children sing Scripture songs in church with all their heart! I was a struggling single mom with two children and newly saved at age 27. I was being convicted in every church service more than once. I was trying to grow as a Christian while my children's dad was totally against my desire to live for God. He tried pulling my children in the opposite direction.

During an extremely difficult time for me, I was very ready to just quit going to church. I sat in one Sunday evening service in church, wondering why I had come, when our pastor began singing Scripture songs. My two children, ages three and five, who had never before sang out loud in church, began to sing the Scripture songs with all their might. I didn't even know they knew the words! – Cindy Kanouse

102

I love ladybugs. When I was a little girl, I found joy in singing the song, "Ladybug, ladybug, fly away home…." When I heard the idea of finding something that reminds me that God loves me, it wasn't ladybugs—at least not at first.

At first it was parking spaces. Then as a pastor's wife, my ladies wanted the opportunity to show their love by buying me reminders of God's love. I still have not found too many pretty ceramic parking spaces, so I chose ladybugs. I can tell dozens of stories of God's using a simple ladybug to remind me that He loves me.

This past December I had surgery twice and almost died. I spent 20 days in the hospital and went home two days before Christmas. I was still bedridden and required in-home nursing care.

One particularly rough, pain-filled Sunday in January after my nurse had left and my family was at church, I found myself all alone. I lay back in my recliner, and something on the light fixture caught my eye. There in January in Iowa when it was 10 degrees outside was one lone little ladybug!

Though my body was weary and pained, my heart swelled with joy at the knowledge that God loved me and wanted me to remember that. He had sent His little messenger to remind me.   – Terri Cannon

103

*I*know God loves me when He shows me something special in His Word I have never before noticed, like opening my understanding of a passage or a phrase. For example, the three emphasized words in Psalm 146:5 could be used for a helpful, encouraging talk. "**Happy** is he that hath the God of Jacob for his **help**, whose **hope** is in the LORD his God."

– Helen MacCormack

104

Ever since I was a little girl, I knew what I wanted to be when I grew up—a wife and a mother. After several years of college, a few broken engagements, and the worry of growing old, I thought my dream or life's plan was not going to happen. I can remember the exact moment when I let go of my desires and turned them 100 percent over to God.

At that time in my life, the Lord gave me complete peace, and I was happy just being me, myself, and I. After a few months the Lord brought a wonderful Christian man into my life whom I married in August of 1988. The Lord used Mrs. Marlene Evans, whom I knew from college (and my future husband knew from her speaking in his father's church) to make the introduction. And my aunt, Loretta Walker, had met my husband's family while traveling to speak at a ladies' conference with Mrs. Evans. These two matchmakers played a part in our wonderful love story, but both my soon-to-be husband and I knew without a doubt that the Lord had brought us together. We are nearing our ninth wedding anniversary this year.

I am reminded of how I feel loved by God not only when I see my husband or when I think of him, but most of all when I see my wedding ring. I not only see the love of my husband, but I always remember how much God loves me and how He gave me the desires of my heart when I truly began trusting Him with all my heart.   – Marsha Schearer

105

In 1998 my husband and I went to Pastors' School at First Baptist Church in Hammond, Indiana, very discouraged. We needed something from God to take home with us to keep going in the church and ministry we had started. We just needed to know He was still with us, that He loved us, and that He knew we were still here trying to serve Him. The week took a nosedive when the phone rang in our motel room around 1:00 a.m. on Thursday morning. My sister, who was a student at Hyles-Anderson College, had to be rushed to the emergency room with pains in her side and back. Since we had our two small children with us, my husband decided that he should go to the hospital and wait with her and that I would go later if she was not released.

My husband returned to our room around 7:00 a.m. with just enough time to get ready for the Thursday morning session. He explained that my sister had several kidney stones and that she had been given some heavy-duty pain medication so she would be asleep for most of the day. I knew that my husband was very exhausted, so I prayed after he left that God would somehow show him that he was loved in a big way. My husband went out to our church van during the dinner break and tried to nap, but he was too tired and very discouraged. (I did not know until later that he had prayed during that break that God would remind him of His love.)

I went to visit my sister and returned just in time for the Thursday evening service. I sat in the Adams Chapel, the overflow chapel with closed circuit monitors for viewing the service, with our son and tried to clear my mind and enjoy the service. Dr. Jack Hyles did something amazing that night. First of all, he asked every pastor to stand who was averaging 100 or less. Then he asked everyone else to put money in the hands and pockets of those pastors. What a blessing!

I couldn't believe what happened next. Brother Hyles began preaching and ranted and raved about starting churches all over this country. Then, he said, "Why don't you be like **Joe Vassak** and go up to New York and carve out a work from nothing like he did?" I couldn't believe his words. I felt so loved when I realized that when Dr. Hyles was preparing his sermon for that night, God brought to his mind a young preacher who needed to have some encouragement and love at that crucial time in his ministry. What a loving God!

– Amy Vassak

106

My husband has a "thing" about pens. He only likes to write with the very nice, expensive pens. He has given me a couple of them, and I have been converted to the "pen snob" club.

Recently, I reached in my purse for my pen, and it was not there. I remembered using it at choir practice the day before and thought, "I must have forgotten to return it to its spot." I figured I would never see it again, and I was rather upset. I have made a practice of not dwelling on things that I cannot change, so I tried to put it out of my mind—after all, it was only a pen.

It was harder for me to forget about than I had expected. Every time I reached for my pen, I would think, "Oh, right, I don't have that anymore." This went on for several days.

Then I had one of those days when nothing went right. I had errands to run that just seemed endless. It was like one of those dreams where you are trying to get to somewhere, but every turn you take is a wrong one.

When I finally arrived home, I was exhausted and still had not done everything I had planned. It was choir practice night, and I still needed to prepare dinner for my husband. When I got out of my car and walked toward my front door, I was tired and discouraged. As I opened the door, the first thing I saw was my pen lying about two feet in front of the door. Since it had been missing for an entire week, I can promise you it had not been lying in front of the door the whole time.

I was so excited to see it! My spirits were lifted immediately, and I thanked God for caring about something as trivial as a pen. Of course, He knew where it was all along, but He chose to reveal it to me at the time when I needed it most.

– Suzan Rust

107

Several years ago the theme for the year in my Sunday school class was "God Loves You!" I wanted each of my girls to choose a love sign from God and to know that He was real to them. Each year I ask my class of eighth grade girls if they have a love sign from God. If I see one of their chosen signs, I think of that girl and am reminded to pray for her. One of my girls this year chose an Aldi grocery cart left in the parking lot. (These carts can be returned to the front of the store and redeemed for a quarter!) One Sunday afternoon on the way home from church, I saw an Aldi grocery cart miles away from the nearest Aldi store. What fun I had sharing the story with this young lady! Of course, when I see someone else's sign, I am reminded that God loves the other person **and** me too! I am greedy about God's love. The pennies, the deer, the hummingbirds...I claim them all!

As a result of choosing this theme for my Sunday school class, I decided to choose my Sunday school girls (current and former) as another love sign from God. I tell the girls in my class that they are a love sign from God to me. Some of them will even greet me with the words "God loves you!" when I see them. Amazingly, the year that I chose this as a love sign from God, Pastor Schaap changed the date for Sunday school promotion from May to August. I have been a member of First Baptist Church of Hammond for over 25 years. That year is the **only** year that teachers had their Sunday school girls for an extra three months! Wow! A three-month long hug from God!

– Rena Fish

108

I was walking to chapel with Kyle McLaughlin, a Hyles-Anderson College student, when we both spotted a penny on the floor. (I don't have a "thing" about most pennies, but I do have a "thing" about wheat pennies.) Kyle said, "Hey, a penny!"

As he picked it up, I said, "It's mine if it's a 'wheatie' because that's how God shows me He loves me."

Kyle looked at it and said, "It's a 'wheatie,' but I picked it up."

I teasingly said, "Well, I guess I'll just have to fight you for it!" He grinned and handed me the penny.

Since that incident, I have been the delighted recipient of several "wheatie" pennies from Kyle. Generally, it's taped to a 3x5 card that he hands to my husband and says, "Would you give this to your wife?" Those pennies have been extra-special to me because a busy college student thinks of me whenever he finds "wheatie" pennies and then goes out of his way to deliver them. God knows just how to make us feel loved—in more ways than one!

P. S. In all fairness to my son-in-law, Hugh McCraney, I must mention that he also watches for "wheaties" and brings them to me. At those times, I feel doubly loved!

– Linda Stubblefield

109

Never give up on God. Sometimes your prayers are answered at the midnight hour. I know, because mine was—literally.

My first grandchild Samantha came from a broken home. She was 13 years old and did not know the Lord. Even though I reared her father in a Christian home, and he was saved and baptized in his youth at First Baptist Church in Hammond,

Indiana, he is now a member of a nondenominational church. Her mother is a non-practicing Catholic. It is in this environment that Samantha began to form her own misguided beliefs about God and religion.

Samantha arrived at our home in Muncie, Indiana, for a week-long visit on June 30, 2007. In great anticipation, I planned a fun-filled week for us. But at the top of my list was her salvation. The week flew by in a flurry of activities. Many times I tried to talk to her about God, but she would tune me out. Her mind was set in the rebellious mode.

As we engaged in small talk, I glanced at the clock and saw that it was midnight. In a few hours Samantha would return to her home in Schererville, Indiana. My heart was heavy because I knew that my time had run out. Little did I know that we were now on God's time.

Just before I turned off her light, she asked me to hand her a small, beautifully decorated vase that was sitting on the top of the dresser. Even though she had placed it there upon her arrival, it had gone virtually unnoticed. When I inquired about the vase, she told me that it contained the ashes of her great-grandmother whom she dearly loved. She said that she always carried it with her because it brought her comfort whenever she was sad or lonely.

"Samantha," I said, "would you like to see your great-grandmother again?"

With tears in her eyes, she said, "Yes, Grandma, I would. Could you show me how?"

Oh, the joy that filled my soul as I led her to Christ at the midnight hour! God is so good! When I didn't know how to reach her, He did. God showed Himself to me in a small vase filled with His divine love! I will never forget the date my granddaughter accepted Jesus as her Lord and Saviour. It was July 6, my dad's birthday! What a blessed gift!

— Crystal Light

110

My daughter was two years old when my husband told me he was going to leave me. We had started a small church in New Jersey, but he had become bitter over the death of his unsaved father. He had resigned from the church, the ministry, and now me. Of course, there was another woman. I did not know it yet, but I was expecting our second child.

One evening I was bathing my daughter and feeling very distraught and burdened. I heard Someone say, *"...I will never leave thee, nor forsake thee."* (Hebrews 13:5) The voice was so real that I spun around to see Who was standing outside my bathroom. There was no one there.

I realized then that it was not an audible voice, but the Lord Himself speaking to my heart. I knew that everything happening to me somehow fit God's plan for me. The Lord spoke to my heart two more times during this terrible period of my life. Believing that God had a plan for my life is what kept me going. God proved His love for me over and over again.

P. S. The baby girl I was expecting will be a junior at Hyles-Anderson College in 2007!

— Patty Ferguson

111

*I*n January 2007 I found out that my father had cancer—the word that nobody ever wants to hear. My dad would have three operations to try to remove the cancer. The third operation was to amputate his left foot. During this time, there were countless doctor's visits, hospital stays, and medications for which to pay. It was a tough time for my family—financially, physically, and emotionally. When the doctors realized that my dad would have to have his foot amputated to stop the spread of cancer, I went through one of the most difficult times in my life. I cried and often asked God "Why?"

For two years I had been taking piano lessons from a lady who is considered one of the best piano teachers in our state. As you can imagine, the lessons were quite expensive. Since the current lessons for the school year were already paid for, I did not really think about them.

When it came time for summer lessons, I needed to come up with $300 to pay for six weeks of lessons. My parents could not afford them, and I had already told them I would be fine if I couldn't take them. The truth was, I really wanted to keep taking lessons. I started to pray, not telling anyone about my need except the Lord. I needed a miracle.

On my seventeenth birthday in May, my piano teacher just happened to call our home to tell me that I wouldn't have a lesson on that day and that it was rescheduled for the next week. My mother told her that would be fine because it was my birthday and I was having a number of friends over for a party. My piano teacher became excited and said, "It's her birthday? Well, let me give her a birthday present too!" She then gave me the summer lessons for FREE! When I found out what she had done, I was so excited. I had received my very first miracle from the Lord. But my miracle got even better.

A week later I received a letter from my piano teacher telling me in writing about free summer tuition. The letter went on to say that she was also giving me a scholarship for the next school year with one-hour weekly lessons—absolutely free! That scholarship alone is worth $2,100. I began to cry because I knew that God loved me so much, and in the midst of my worries and fears over Dad's cancer, He reached down and gave me a miracle to let me know that He was real!

My dad always says that God only works miracles for those who need them! I really needed to know that God loved me, and He certainly proved His love in a BIG way.

– Anna Bish

112

God showed me that He loved me by not letting me break down in the middle of the night while driving by myself. When I was newly saved, I was on my way home from a very long trip. About two and a half hours away from home at midnight, I noticed smoke slowly and steadily coming from under the hood of my van. I was afraid that if it stopped for anything, the van wouldn't start again. I began to pray for God to please get me home without breaking down. I arrived in my driveway at 2:30

a.m., and the moment I turned off the van, the smoke poured out and some kind of fluid leaked everywhere.

The next morning was Sunday. I woke up, got ready for church, prayed the whole time that the van would start, and it did! I made it to church and to a friend's house afterward. The van did need some work, and I know only God could have helped me get home and then to church the next day!

– Cindy Kanouse

113

My husband Eric and I, along with a couple from our church, Josh and Jenny Musser, were able to spend a wonderful and relaxing time in the Reno/Lake Tahoe area in Nevada and California. While we were on vacation, we hiked a trail back in the mountains to a place called Eagle Lake. You would never know that lake even exists for you cannot see it from a road. You can only get there on foot. It is surrounded by mountainous cliffs and huge pine trees. There is a small island in the middle of the lake. We sat on a fallen log where the lake flows into the stream that leads to Eagle Falls. We all just sat there soaking in the beauty and tranquility of the moment and the place.

Having used all our water on the hike there, we even filled our water bottles and drank from the cool mountain stream. I was in Heaven for it is probably my most favorite spot in the entire world. Then God dropped down a little sign from above just to say—"Remember Me? I am the One Who created this spot—these mountains, this lake, this beauty!"

I looked over and on a nearby bush, I saw a beautiful mountain bluebird. Josh even fed it several of our nuts that we had been snacking on while sitting and taking in the majesty around us. Each time the bluebird would take the nut from Josh, fly away, and then come back for another one. Near the end of our stay, he brought back a friend—two beautiful mountain bluebirds from God! Yes, God loves me! God loves us!

– Rebekah Tastet

114

In the spring of 2004 I found a lump in my left breast. I was in the doctor's office three days later listening to her tell me that I needed to have a sonogram and a possible biopsy. I went to the hospital the following week for the sonogram, and the doctor said that she could tell by the shape and the size that it was cancer. She scheduled me for a biopsy to confirm her diagnosis, and I left the office in a fog. I drove to Main Street in our town, pulled into a parking space, and sobbed. I prayed and asked God to please help my family go through this trial.

We held an annual conference at our church in June, and some great men of God were there. They anointed me with oil and prayed for me. My biopsy was scheduled for the Wednesday following the conference. While my husband drove the preachers to the airport, I went to the hospital to have my biopsy.

The nurse handed me the "lovely" gown with the drafty back and I quickly changed, but I couldn't bring myself to leave the bathroom. I prayed for a bomb threat…it did not happen. Finally, the nurse knocked on the bathroom door and asked if I was okay. I reluctantly came out and told her that I was very scared and nervous.

She told me not to worry and then said, "I have to do another sonogram first just to make sure we know right where the tumor is. You never know, you might not need a biopsy."

I laughed and said, "Yeah, right!"

She started the sonogram and didn't say anything for a few minutes. Then she asked me if she was viewing the correct one. I said that she was. She excused herself for a minute and returned with my original sonogram. She tried once again to get a picture. Finally, I worked up my nerve to ask her what was the matter. She said that she couldn't find a tumor. I started to cry. She told me to stop because she was going to get the doctor on call, and he would think she had upset me.

She returned a few minutes later with the doctor who had her redo the sonogram while he watched the monitor. Although I couldn't tell anything from the screen, it was soon very clear to me by the looks on their faces that the tumor was nowhere to be found! I left the hospital that day amazingly convinced of God's love for me!   – Amy Vassak

115

At 35 my husband suffered a brain aneurysm. While he lay in the ICU at the University of Chicago in a drug-induced coma, I awoke daily at 4:00 a.m. to sob for hours before I would get ready for work. After ten days, I prayed as I sat in the La-Z-Boy recliner looking out the sliding glass door. "Father," I prayed, "please let me know that no matter what the outcome that I will be okay. Help me to know our young son will be okay. Whatever the outcome, Father…I beg You… assure me."

Then after months of spring and summer and the appearance of not one single American goldfinch—my favorite bird—one appeared on the stoop of my sliding glass door. Nothing was there for him to eat, and there was no reason for him to come and sit, yet he did. He sat, for what seemed an eternity, staring into my window. My loving God had made sure I got the message—it would all be okay. My husband did die, but he went Home to Jesus. Years later I remarried a godly, loving, gentle man and have a wonderful second marriage.

Now as I ride my bike or take a walk and a goldfinch flies by, I know it will all be okay. It may hurt, but I will grow, and it will all be okay. My Father loves me…and is so good to show me!   – Kelly Oney

116

Around 3:00 a.m. on the second Friday of October 2001, my husband awoke to the sound of a loud pop. He looked out of our bedroom window and discovered that our neighbor's car was on fire. The front of the car was parked right next to the garage door, so the garage was also beginning to burn. Brother Schaap called 911, then asked me to call the neighbors while he got dressed.

The lady of the house answered the phone. I could tell that I had awakened her. "Pat, your car is on fire, and it is parked right at the garage door. Please be sure to get everyone out of the house right away." I repeated myself to be sure that Pat had understood.

My husband got our fire extinguisher from our basement and headed to our neighbor's house. Our daughter Jaclynn had gotten up, and she and I sat on the porch and watched my husband put out the fire. The fire extinguisher didn't work, so he tried the neighbor's hose. By the time the three fire trucks arrived on the scene, the fire was out.

After the fire was extinguished, it was discovered that most of the fire in the garage had traveled to the wall closest to the house. My husband had definitely saved the lives of this family. There was even damage to some of the items that were in the entrance of the house nearest to the garage.

Saturday morning I felt the Lord urging me to go next door and witness to our neighbors. I really wanted my husband to go, but he was at the church. Our neighbors work long hours, he as a lawyer and she as a nurse at the University of Chicago Hospitals (where my father passed away). I feared I would not find them home for another week if I did not go. Besides, something (or Someone) inside me kept telling me that if I did not walk through this door, God would not save our neighbors for whom we had been praying.

My soul-winning partner arrived at my house around noon. "Guess what?" I said, "I would like to go soul winning next door today." We did not go because we were bold. She was nervous, and I was nervous. Yet I saw my partner fake boldness and encourage me to go. I felt ten times more bold with her by my side.

I knocked on the door, and Pat answered. She led us to her kitchen table where we chatted several minutes about the fire. I tried to express my sympathy for her.

Then I said something like this, "Pat, I know why God woke my husband and had him put out that fire. God wanted me to come over and ask you this question, 'If you had died in that fire, are you 100 percent sure you would have gone to Heaven?'"

With tears literally streaming down her face, Pat accepted Christ as her Saviour. My partner's eyes and mine were moist with tears.

"I have been wanting to get a Bible and read it," Pat said. "That is not something the Catholic church encourages, you know." Then she added, "Do you mean that if I trust Jesus once, I can know I am going to Heaven? I thought this was something I had to do over and over again, just hoping that I had done it soon enough before my death to be forgiven."

"No, Pat," I replied. "You don't have to live in that kind of bondage anymore. You only have to trust Jesus once. If you died having unconfessed sins, you would still go to Heaven." The tears flowed, and Pat seem relieved. I felt I was watching a soul set free.

Pat's husband Bill came into the room. He is a little more aloof in personality, so I was fearful to witness to him. However, I walked through the next door of opportunity, and Bill was also saved. My husband's reply to the neighbors' salvation? "God has provided the illustration for my sermon on Sunday." The next Sunday was the first Sunday of our Fall Program, Firemen Sunday.

A couple of weeks later, my husband presented Pat and Bill with two leather Scofield Bibles with their names engraved on each one. Now Pat was saved, Bill was saved, and their son Matt was saved. Our children had led Matt to the Lord during a Bible club they had at our house as children. There was only one family member left. Fifteen-year-old Katie had never been saved. She is quite a bit younger than our children and did not attend our Bible club.

I began to pray daily that the Lord would set us up to see Katie saved. (He had set me up so beautifully before, I'm afraid I put most of the responsibility on Him.) Katie was out of town visiting relatives for several weeks, but daily I prayed that Katie would be saved. I had also been praying that God would give me a special soul-winning experience as a Christmas gift to my dad now in Heaven.

Two days before Christmas, I asked Jaclynn to take some cookies and a card to several of our neighbors. This is a tradition in which Jaclynn loves to be a part. Almost on a whim, it hit me. "Jaclynn, Katie may be back for the holidays. Perhaps you can witness to her when you take the cookies to her family."

Sure enough, about an hour later, Jaclynn informed me that Katie had been saved in her living room as her family looked on. The true Spirit of Christmas seemed so real to us that night, and I felt very loved by God.

My husband and I had been praying diligently that our neighbors would be saved. We have seen four of them saved in 2001. We are praying that God will save more of them in 2002.

May I share with you some lessons from this experience?

- **God loves to show His power and to get involved with our lives.** With all of our hearts, Brother Schaap and I believe God allowed my husband to put out the fire to encourage him about the Fall Program.
- **God works on desire.** I had just begun to really desire my neighbors to be saved. I prayed with desire, and God seemed to do the rest.
- **When we walk through open doors, God opens more.**
- **God is willing to set us up as soul winners.** This does not mean we should not do "cold-turkey" soul winning. We do this type of soul winning regularly. But I am asking God daily to "set us up" to win more neighbors, and I am definitely looking for opportunities.
- **A soul-winning partner is as important to God as the soul winner.** I cannot tell you how much I appreciated my partner for "faking" boldness and giving me courage that day.
- **God loves to show Himself to those who are grieving.** He showed Himself to me in two ways:

First of all, I did not realize until after Pat was saved that she had been a nurse at the hospital where Dad had passed away. Her salvation was even sweeter when she said as I left her home, "I'm sorry about your dad. Did you know he was one of our patients?"

Secondly, I hate to admit it, but I had been praying for snow for Christmas. On December 23, right after Katie got saved, the first snow of the season came and covered all of the ground just in time for Christmas. Our Christmas lights on the roof of our house, which had gone out for several days, mysteriously came back on at the same time. You say coincidence? I say God! If you are grieving, look for God's love. He wants to show Himself to you. Also, I hope you'll consider being a soul winner this year. God has so much He would like to show those of you who are soul winners!

Just like our neighbors, you too can know 100% for sure, without a doubt, that you can go to Heaven. You need to know the following:

- Realize there is none good. Romans 3:10 says, *"As it is written, There is none righteous, no, not one."*
- See yourself as a sinner. Romans 3:23 says, *"For all have sinned, and come short of the glory of God."*
- Recognize where sin came from. Romans 5:12 says, *"Wherefore, as by one man sin entered into the world, and death by sin; and so death passed upon all men, for that all have sinned."*
- Notice God's price on sin. Romans 6:23 says, *"For the wages of sin is death; but the gift of God is eternal life through Jesus Christ our Lord."*
- Realize that Christ died for you. Romans 5:8 says, *"But God commendeth his love toward us, in that, while we were yet sinners, Christ died for us."*
- Take God at His Word. Romans 10:13 says, *"For whosoever shall call upon the name of the Lord shall be saved."*

- Claim God's promise for your salvation. Romans 10:9-11 says, *"That if thou shalt confess with thy mouth the Lord Jesus, and shalt believe in thine heart that God hath raised him from the dead, thou shalt be saved. For with the heart man believeth unto righteousness; and with the mouth confession is made unto salvation. For the scripture saith, Whosoever believeth on him shall not be ashamed."*

Now pray. Confess that you are a sinner. Ask God to save you and receive Christ as your personal Saviour.

– Cindy Schaap

Subject Index

Index of Authors